THE KOREAN MINORITY IN JAPAN

Richard H. Mitchell

UNIVERSITY OF CALIFORNIA PRESS
BERKELEY AND LOS ANGELES / 1967

University of California Press
Berkeley and Los Angeles, California

Cambridge University Press
London, England

Copyright © 1967,
by The Regents of the University of California
Library of Congress Catalog Card Number: 67–18074
Printed in the United States of America

To Yoshiko

PREFACE

The numerous modern studies of East Asian problems include several excellent treatments of the events that led to Japan's annexation of Korea in 1910, but little has been written about the occupation which followed and the relationship between the Koreans and the Japanese. The Japanese conquest of Korea had a profound influence on the subsequent history of both countries, yet this important subject has been neglected by American, Korean, and Japanese historians. During the last decade, only a small number of Japanese scholars have encouraged the study of Korean history in a few Japanese universities. Korean scholars, despite their advantage of knowing both Korean and Japanese, have made even less effort than the Japanese to study Japanese-Korean relations.

The Japanese expansion, and the Korean response, during the Meiji period of 1868 to 1911, bound the two nations into an often unhappy but nevertheless intimate association for half a century. The study of the modern history of one country, therefore, must include that of the other. To a lesser extent this is true also of the postwar era.

The Korean Minority in Japan

Over twenty years have passed since the end of the Second World War, but it has been difficult for Korea and Japan to settle their basic disputes and restore normal diplomatic relations. Because of problems which have persisted into contemporary times, it is necessary, for any solution to be effective to examine some of the past and present causes of the impasse.

This study analyzes only one small part of the complex pattern of modern Japanese-Korean relations, the long-standing and continuing problem of the Korean minority in Japan. This minority of nearly 600,000 is a legacy from Japan's period of imperialistic expansion. The purpose of this study is to trace the development of the Korean minority, and to analyze the controversies that arose between the immigrants and the Japanese. Koreans in Japan played an important role in developing Korean nationalism and in starting the March First Movement of 1919 in Korea. An active communist element within the Korean minority of Japan joined forces with the Japanese Communist Party in 1929. During the next several years of communist activity in Japan, the Korean communists gradually rose in the ranks of the party until by 1933, no important decision could be made without consulting them. They used Japan as a base of operations in their unsuccessful attempt to rebuild the Communist Party in Korea, and their propaganda aroused the suspicions of Japanese officials. This only led to stepped-up police surveillance of all Korean nationalist activities.

A key issue in current Korean-Japanese negotiations for normalization of diplomatic relations was the status of the Korean minority in Japan. These negotiations were not successful until agreement was achieved on the legal status of the minority. To understand other current problems, such as the voluntary repatriation of more than 80,000 Ko-

Preface

reans from Japan to the Democratic People's Republic of Korea, the relations between the minority and the Japanese must be examined. In this study of the problem, extensive use has been made for the first time of Japanese government records, especially those of the Home Ministry, which reveal the extent of the tensions between the two peoples.

In the transliteration of Japanese and Korean names, the standard form is used, with the family name first, except for some well-known forms, such as "Syngman Rhee." Bars are used to mark the long vowels in Japanese, and generally the McCune-Reischauer system has been followed for the transliteration of Korean. For common words, such as Tokyo and Osaka, the long vowels are not marked.

I should like to express my gratitude to those who have contributed to the publication of this book. I am grateful to the East Asian Studies Committee at the University of Wisconsin, which supplied the funds for an uninterrupted year of research and writing. I am indebted to Professor Eugene P. Boardman, who encouraged me to do this study; to Professor Leonard Gordon, for his careful reading and valuable suggestions; to Mrs. Yukiko Blaschko and Matsuda Yasuhiko, who provided important information in the form of personal interviews; to the University of California Press for editorial assistance; to Miss Marguerite Christensen, General Reference Department, Memorial Library, the University of Wisconsin; and to the library staff of the International House of Japan. I think it best not to mention by name the numerous Koreans in Japan and in Korea who furnished documents and rendered other aid, but I wish to express my gratitude for their help. I owe a special debt to Yoshiko, for her double duty as a research assistant and wife.

R.H.M.

CONTENTS

I   *Relations Between Korea and Japan Until 1910*   1

II   *Korean Students and the March First Movement*   14

III   *Origins of the Korean Minority Problem, 1920–1930*   27

IV   *The Communist and Nationalist Movements: The First Phase*   48

V   *The Communist and Nationalist Movements: The Second Phase*   59

VI   *The Effect of Japan's War Efforts on the Korean Migrants*   75

VII   *Problems of Assimilation*   90

VIII *The Korean Minority in Occupied Japan, 1945–1952*   100

 IX *The Korean Minority in "New Japan," 1952–1960*   119

  X *The Unification Issue: The Intensification of Political Activity, 1960–1963*   145

 XI *The Future of the Minority*   157

    Bibliography   165

    Index   177

I
RELATIONS BETWEEN KOREA AND JAPAN UNTIL 1910

The origins of the early Japanese remain obscure, but the ethnic traits of the peoples of the islands and those of the Korean peninsula show marked similarities. Their languages, for example, are closely related and are both very different from Chinese. Especially during the early historical period, the relationship between western Japan and southern Korea "remained very close, and there was not much to distinguish them from one another."[1]

The first political unification of Japan, during the third or fourth century A.D., was accelerated by the Yamato clan's close contacts with Korea. Missions from Korea brought the arts of writing, painting, and casting metal to the islands, along with a sophisticated religion, Buddhism, and political concepts and administrative forms, all learned from the Chinese. From at least the beginning of the Christian Era,

[1] George Sansom, *A History of Japan to 1334*, I, 15.

Koreans and Chinese went to Japan to escape the dynastic wars of the peninsula and the turmoil in China; and as early as the fourth century, whole villages migrated to Japan. Most of the new arrivals were skilled in a trade or a craft, or were farmers who knew the secrets of silkworm culture. The Japanese, eager to learn these advanced techniques, treated the immigrants well.[2]

During the fifth and sixth centuries, Japan's domestic politics were closely tied to events in Korea, where Japan was involved in the conflict among the kingdoms of Paekche, Silla, and Koguryŏ. Each of the three kingdoms attempted to form an alliance with a second and to eliminate the third. Japan tried to exploit this situation to her advantage through military alliances, often sealed by marriage, with one or the other of the three kingdoms.[3]

In 552, the king of Paekche requested military aid from Japan and sent a bronze image of Buddha and several volumes of Buddhist scriptures to the Japanese court.[4] Though Japan sent aid, Paekche was overrun by Silla during the following century, and the Japanese were pushed out of the small area they had long influenced on the southeastern tip of the peninsula.[5] When Paekche was defeated in 662–663 by the combined arms of Silla and T'ang China, thousands of Paekcheans fled to Japan. Many of these refugees came from the defeated state's upper class, and others pos-

[2] Sansom, *Japan: A Short Cultural History*, pp. 43–44.
[3] Sansom, *A History of Japan to 1334*, pp. 15, 34.
[4] *Ibid.*, p. 47.
[5] Edwin O. Reischauer and John K. Fairbank, *East Asia the Great Tradition*, I, 406, 407–10, 468. Some historians say that Japan never dominated an area in southeastern Korea. For example, see Suk Hyung Kim, *et al., On the Grave Errors in the Descriptions on Korea of the "World History" Edited by the U.S.S.R. Academy of Sciences,* pp. 12–17.

sessed some technical skill,[6] but this migration during the seventh century was essentially a continuation of the previous ones from the mainland to Japan. By the early ninth century, more than a third of the families of the central Japanese nobility were descendants of these Korean and Chinese immigrants.[7]

The Koreans introduced the Japanese to Buddhism and the arts closely associated with this Indian religion. Many of the early religious statues in Japan were obviously imported from Korea or were the work of immigrant craftsmen. Buddhist images in Japan which date back to the seventh century are almost identical with those of the same period which are found on the peninsula. One of the most famous, and perhaps the most beautiful, is a standing wooden figure of the bodhisattva of mercy and compassion, which is preserved at the Hōryūji near Nara, Japan. Reflecting Korean influences, it is still referred to as the "Kudara Kannon" (Paekche Kannon).[8]

During the fourth, fifth, and sixth centuries the population of Japan was still heterogeneous, and the full assimilation of the Korean immigrants was possible because Japan had not yet evolved into a fully centralized state. The unpacified tribes in the southwest and northeast, the Kumaso and the Ainu, preserved their distinct characteristics. Even the Yamato, who populated part of the central island, were far from being homogeneous.[9] Korean immigrants could establish themselves quite easily in Japan in this period, but they were greeted with mild prejudice even then.[10]

[6] Reischauer and Fairbank, *East Asia the Great Tradition*, I, 471. Evelyn McCune, *The Arts of Korea*, p. 66.
[7] Sansom, *Japan: A Short Cultural History*, p. 44.
[8] Hugo Munsterberg, *The Arts of Japan*, pp. 18, 19, 24–25, 27.
[9] Sansom, *Japan: A Short Cultural History*, p. 43.
[10] Shigeaki Ninomiya, "An Inquiry Concerning the Origin, Development, and Present Situation of the *Eta* in Relation to the History

A Change in Attitudes

During the centuries that followed, the relationship between the Koreans and the Japanese changed from that of a teacher instructing a novice in the rudiments of civilized living to that of competing states. The Japanese soon turned directly to China for their inspiration, and a series of missions plied back and forth between the islands and the Chinese mainland.[11] Gradually, however, the Japanese acquired enough intellectual sophistication to develop a culture of their own, so the great embassies to China were terminated after 838. Japan lapsed into a period of near isolation as it became less hospitable to peoples from overseas. During these same centuries Korea also underwent profound changes. The country was unified for the first time by Silla during the 660's and Japanese influence was excluded.

Between the Nara period (710–784) and the latter part of the nineteenth century, the people of the two nations gradually became estranged. The exact cause of this development is uncertain, but it is clear that during these centuries the Korean nation underwent a very different historical experience from that of the Japanese. The Korean government patterned itself closely on the Chinese model in which the Confucian ethical system strongly influenced the mores of the court and higher level civil service. On the other hand, the Japanese followed another path and passed through a feudal experience strikingly similar to that of western Europe. Furthermore, nationalism emerged much earlier and grew more rapidly in Japan than in Korea.

Two developments that occurred during these centuries indelibly marked Korean–Japanese relations until the twen-

of Social Classes in Japan," *Transactions of the Asiatic Society of Japan*, X, Second Series (December, 1933), 69–70.

[11] Reischauer and Fairbank, *East Asia the Great Tradition*, I, 476–78.

tieth century. First came the activities of the wakō (Japanese pirates) and then the invasion of Korea by Toyotomi Hideyoshi, the paramount military figure of Japan.

The wakō began as small, poorly organized groups in the thirteenth century and then developed into large, well-organized bands supported by powerful Japanese lords. Ready to engage in either legitimate trade or piracy, whichever seemed to suit the situation, they were based in western Japan but operated throughout eastern Asia. Most of their raids were along the Korean and Chinese coasts. One Korean official traveling to Japan estimated that more than a thousand Japanese vessels and tens of thousands of men were engaged in piracy. During the fourteenth century Korea bore the main brunt of their raids, and much of the Korean coast became a barren wasteland.[12]

Support of piracy was not a policy of the central Japanese government, which was itself torn by constant internal strife during the fourteenth and fifteenth centuries and could not control the lords of western Japan. The wakō were not all Japanese. Koreans and Chinese also became members of the bands and pillaged along the Korean coasts,[13] but the Japanese were blamed for the raids. Even in modern Korea there is animosity directed against the Japanese for those devastating incursions.

Korea was invaded in 1592 by the forces of Toyotomi Hideyoshi as the first step in his grand plan to conquer China. Because it lay between Hideyoshi and his goal, Korea served as the battleground for the war between Japan and the Ming dynasty. The Japanese army advanced far into northern Korea, and some troops even reached Chinese territory. During seven years of intermittent warfare, large

---

[12] Delmer M. Brown, *Money Economy in Medieval Japan*, p. 18.
[13] *Ibid.*, p. 17.

parts of the peninsula were devastated. The Korean people suffered at the hands of both the Japanese and Chinese forces. The war ended when Hideyoshi died in 1598 and the Japanese army in Korea was evacuated.[14] But the memory of that Seven Years' War poisoned relations between the two nations for many centuries.

Hideyoshi was succeeded by Tokugawa Ieyasu (d. 1616), who reversed the previous expansionist policies and directed his energies to completing the unification of Japan. Tokugawa established a family dynasty that controlled Japan for two and a half centuries.

Relations between the two nations during this period were uneventful. Congratulatory missions were exchanged by each new Korean king and each Japanese shogun, and limited trade was carried on through the island of Tsushima.[15] During this period, however, the Tokugawa shogunate remolded Japanese society and divided its people into rigid social classes. This closed social structure, in which every person was assigned a place, had no room for outsiders.[16]

The Korea Problem

Geography, which had always played an inordinately important role in Korean history, helped decide the fate of

[14] The Japanese mobilized a striking force of nearly 200,000 men for the attack. This gigantic military effort was carefully planned, and a reserve of about 100,000 was stationed near Nagoya where Hideyoshi had his headquarters. For details see George Sansom, "The Invasion of Korea," *A History of Japan, 1334–1615*, II, 352–362. Hideyoshi resigned as regent in 1592; however, until his death he remained the dominant political and military leader.

[15] Hilary Conroy, *The Japanese Seizure of Korea, 1868–1910*, pp. 21–22. Korea was the only nation with which Japan had diplomatic relations during the period of seclusion. See Yoshi S. Kuno, *Japanese Expansion on the Asiatic Continent*, II, 327–343.

[16] Douglas G. Haring, "Japanese National Character," reprinted

Korea in the nineteenth century. Caught between China, Russia, and Japan, the country became the battleground of stronger powers. Korea was controlled by a conservative Confucian hierarchy which looked backward to Korea's magnificent cultural past. The government refused to accept the changing conditions of the modern world and responded to the challenge of Western expansion by maintaining a rigid policy of seclusion.

In contrast, Japan's response to the nineteenth century was completely different. The Japanese engaged in a flurry of activity to "modernize" their nation by consciously copying advanced Western technology. Perhaps as an outlet for their own anxiety to keep pace with Western industrialization, many Japanese looked down on the Koreans, who seemed unable to transform their country into a modern nation. The Chōsen mondai (Korea problem) greatly concerned Japanese of various political persuasions who saw Korea as a security problem, as an area for economic penetration, or as an opportunity to help modernize another Asian country.

Not all Koreans, however, rejected the modern world. Some realized that foreign knowledge might be useful, if only for military defense. A few members of the Korean ruling class, reformers like Kim Ok-kyun and Pak Yŏng-hyo, attempted to change the reactionary policies of the Yi dynasty government. Japan provided a graphic example of what might be done in Korea and acted as a magnet to these eager men who wanted to learn the secrets of Western power. Japanese liberals like Fukuzawa Yukichi, who encouraged these progressive Koreans and introduced them to Western ideas of nationalism and reform, "saw Japan inau-

in Bernard S. Silberman (ed.), *Japanese Character and Culture*, pp. 387-399.

gurating a new day in Korea much as the United States had done in Japan."[17]

Kim Ok-kyun and other Korean reformers received most of their information about the modern world from Japanese texts and study in Japan. A number of Japanese aided the Korean reformers and students during the same period. Fukuzawa Yukichi opened his home to Korean students while they attended school in Japan and encouraged other Japanese to help the Korean students.[18] Kim Ok-kyun, who later became leader of the progressive faction in Korea, attended Fukuzawa's private school and was one of the first Koreans to acquire knowledge of Western economics, politics, geography and history.[19] After his return to Korea, Kim started a plan to send Koreans to Japan for study. In 1881 he persuaded the king to approve his proposal, and sixty-one students were sent. The young men spent their first six months studying Japanese, then divided into small groups and went to various schools.[20] Kim became increasingly involved in politics, and when the conservatives failed to follow his reform program he attempted a coup but was defeated and forced to flee Korea.[21]

Korea signed her first modern treaty, the Treaty of Kanghwa, in 1876. A Korean embassy was sent to Japan,[22] but by the early 1890's xenophobia was rising in Korea where the

[17] John K. Fairbank, Edwin O. Reischauer, and Albert M. Craig, *East Asia the Modern Transformation*, II, 466.
[18] Hilary Conroy, "Chōsen Mondai: The Korean Problem in Meiji Japan," *Proceedings of the American Philosophical Society*, C (1956), 445.
[19] Clarence N. Weems, Jr., "The Korean Reform and Independence Movement (1881–1898)," (unpublished doctoral dissertation), p. 23.
[20] Weems, "The Korean Reform and Independence Movement (1881–1898)," p. 26. Channing Liem, *America's Finest Gift to Korea: The Life of Philip Jaisohn*, p. 17.
[21] Fairbank, *East Asia the Modern Transformation*, p. 466.
[22] Clarence N. Weems, Jr. (ed.), *Hulbert's History of Korea*, II, 221.

Japanese were singled out as targets. The Korean government's official policy of seclusion had heightened these feelings, and exploitation of Koreans by the Japanese merchants who flocked to Korea after the Treaty of Kanghwa had stimulated it.[23] In 1893, the Tonghak Rebellion took place and Koreans rallied to the slogan, "Reject Japan and repel the foreigners." [24] The Tonghak, a nationalistic religious group, had most of its strength south of Seoul in an area which had a population with strong feelings against Japan.[25] Although three centuries had elapsed since the Hideyoshi invasion, many clans in Kyongsang Province still thought of Japan as the enemy of Korea.[26] The Tonghak leaders branded the Japanese as brigands with a "warlike heart," and planned to destroy them and all other foreigners.[27]

The Korean minister of education shared the feelings of his Tonghak subjects. While still in office he published a book in which he noted, "The Japanese live in the east sea, the people are of a bad, savage disposition, delight in conquering others, and take life lightly." [28] The Korean government helped to keep the memory of Hideyoshi's invasion alive by holding a celebration in December, 1893, to commemorate the tercentenary of "driving out" the Japanese.[29]

[23] Chong-Sik Lee, "The Korean Nationalist Movement, 1905-1945" (unpublished doctorial dissertation), p. 85.
[24] "The Japanese were more particularly the object of Tonghak hatred than the other foreigners. Tonghak posters, which specified Japanese (Wa) separately from other foreigners (Yō), may be evidence of this." Conroy, *The Japanese Seizure of Korea*, p. 232. Also see Lee, "The Korean Nationalist Movement, 1905-1945," p. 80. The Tonghak ("Eastern Learning") movement is succinctly explained in Fairbank, *East Asia the Modern Transformation*, pp. 463-464, 466-467.
[25] Lee, "The Korean Nationalist Movement, 1905-1945," p. 84.
[26] *Ibid.*
[27] *Ibid.*, p. 82.
[28] *The Korean Repository*, 1896, p. 421.
[29] Conroy, *The Japanese Seizure of Korea*, p. 206.

The Japanese-supported reform program, started by progressives like Kim Ok-kyun, resulted only in "tremendous resistance to Japan and the reform ideas."[30] Japanese involvement in the assassination of Korea's Queen Min and the murder of Resident-general Itō in 1909 by a Korean added to the rapidly accumulating legacy of mutual hatred. Thousands of Japanese, many of them hoping to acquire wealth, poured into Korea during the closing years of the nineteenth century. The relationship between these "irresponsible adventurers" and the Koreans was strained.[31]

Despite increased friction between the two nations, Korean students eager for knowledge continued to travel to Japan. The majority reached Tokyo, and by 1907 there were five hundred in the capital city. Some were supported by the Korean government, some by the Korean imperial household, a few by Japanese schools, and the rest by private means.[32]

The Annexation of Korea

At the end of the nineteenth century, the struggle between the imperialist powers intensified. Japan responded by asserting her dominant position in Korea, first by removing the peninsula from China's sphere of influence and then by frustrating Russia's expansionist policy. Although Japan's motives for annexing Korea remain unclear, it is certain that more and more influential Japanese became convinced that total annexation was Japan's only real solution to the "Korea problem."[33]

[30] Weems, "The Korean Reform and Independence Movement (1881–1898)," p. 110.
[31] Kanichi Asakawa, "Japan and Korea," *The Dartmouth Bi-Monthly*, I (1906), 33.
[32] D. G. Green (ed.), *The Christian Movement in Japan*, p. 159.
[33] For an interesting review of this problem see "Japanese Imperial-

Korea and Japan Until 1910

The outbreak of the Russo-Japanese War in February, 1904, provided Japan with an excuse to invade Korea, force the ruler of Korea to sign a treaty of alliance, establish a "modified" protectorate over Korea, and occupy the peninsula.[34] After this action, the process of complete Japanese control of the Korean government rapidly accelerated. Korean foreign affairs came under Japan's formal control on November 17, 1905, and the Japanese were empowered to appoint a resident-general at Seoul to advise the Korean king. Itō Hirobumi was the first. When the Japanese discussed a new and more comprehensive treaty in 1907, the king abdicated rather than agree. His son, however, was forced to negotiate a new convention on July 25, 1907, which made Korea a full protectorate. This process of gradual encroachment was brought to its ultimate conclusion on August 22, 1910, when the country was finally annexed by Japan.[35]

The Japanese conquest of Korea did not proceed without a Korean protest. Korean students in Japan, inflamed by the forced abdication of their king, held meetings and denounced Japan. Congregating at the former Korean legation, one group stated that it would be better to die than to accept the abdication.[36] In Korea also, the Japanese met considerable protest. The order of August 1, 1907, for the disbanding of the Korean army set off a riot among members of the Korean First Battalion in Seoul. Disorder quickly spread throughout the country. Resident-general Itō's deputy chief of general affairs, Tsuruhara, wrote that it was quiet during the day but that fighting occurred each

ism and Aggression: Reconsiderations. I.," *The Journal of Asian Studies*, XXII (August, 1963), 469-472.
[34] Hugh Borton, *Japan's Modern Century*, pp. 240-241.
[35] *Ibid.*, pp. 244-249.
[36] Conroy, *The Japanese Seizure of Korea*, pp. 362-363.

night, and that anti-Japanese feeling was very strong.[37] Itō himself noted that anti-Japanese feeling was increasing.[38] From 1907 to 1911, a series of Korean uprisings, quelled by the Japanese, caused the death of nearly 18,000 Koreans, and attempts by Koreans to assassinate Korean collaborators and Japanese officials were common.[39] The Japanese referred to the dead Koreans as "rioters," but from the numbers killed, it would appear that some clashes reached the proportion of small battles.

The Japanese army carried out the final annexation of Korea in 1910 and ruled the country for nearly a decade under a military dictatorial government. Although the first governor-general, General Terauchi Masatake, stated that the goal of Japan in Korea was "complete harmony and assimilation," [40] Nothing in the seven-article treaty of annexation guaranteed the equality of the Koreans with the Japanese.[41] Immediately after the annexation, the Japanese military government, ignoring the nationalist feelings of the Koreans, initiated a policy of forced assimilation designed to "Japanize" the entire population. The teaching of the Korean language and history was forbidden, the Korean press was silenced, and any patriot who challenged the new regime was jailed or executed.[42]

Writing in 1905, one historian stated, "It would be very hard to find a Korean child who does not drink in, almost with his mother's milk, a feeling of dislike against the Japa-

[37] *Ibid.*, p. 367.
[38] *Ibid.*, p. 364.
[39] Chong-sik Lee, *The Politics of Korean Nationalism*, p. 81.
[40] George Trumbull Ladd, "The Annexation of Korea: An Essay in 'Benevolent Assimilation,'" *The Yale Review*, New Series, I (1911–1912), 655.
[41] Henry Chung (ed.), *Treaties and Conventions between Corea and Other Powers*, pp. 225–226.
[42] For details see Lee, "Japanese Rule: The First Phase," *The Politics of Korean Nationalism*, pp. 89–100.

nese. On the other hand, the Japanese seem to have imbibed as strong a feeling toward the Koreans." [43] The feeling was one of contempt. The beginning of the colonial period between Korea and Japan was far from auspicious. The peninsula was soaked in blood and new hatreds were generated to add to the traditional ones.

[43] *The Korea Review*, 1905, p. 161. See also Weems, Hulbert's History of Korea, I, 349, and Kuno, *Japanese Expansion on the Asiatic Continent*, I, 342.

II
KOREAN STUDENTS AND THE MARCH FIRST MOVEMENT

For several years after the 1910 annexation of Korea, the size of the Korean minority in Japan remained very small; it was not until the latter part of the First World War that Korean laborers came to Japan in large numbers. There were, however, several hundred Korean students in Japan who were especially receptive to the liberal ideas of Japanese and foreign origin.[1] Tokyo had become the intel-

[1] See Japan, Gaimushō, *Taishō jūyonen chūni okeru zairyū Chōsenjin no jōkyō*, Library of Congress Reel SP47, Special Studies 155, p. 212. Hereafter referred to as SP155.

Date	Koreans in Japan	Date	Koreans in Japan
1913	3,635	1917	14,502
1916	5,624	1919	26,605

These figures do not include students: in 1907 there were about 500, and between 1909 and 1920 about 700. See D. G. Green (ed.), *The Christian Movement in Japan*, p. 159; and Chong-sik Lee, "The Korean Nationalist Movement, 1905–1945" (unpublished doctoral dissertation), p. 279.

lectual center of eastern Asia to which Chinese and Korean students were drawn to study the philosophy and the industrial techniques of Western civilization.[2]

Korea did not have enough colleges, or even high schools, to satisfy the needs of students hungry for the new knowledge. The Confucian-style schools of the Yi dynasty (1392–1910) were either suppressed by the Japanese after annexation or were forced to close for other reasons. The high schools established by the Japanese could not begin to absorb all the Korean students who wished to attend. The Japanese Government High School in Seoul, for example, had nearly 4,000 applicants who wanted to study the Western ideas introduced by Japan, but only 200 could be admitted.[3] Young Koreans who could afford it traveled to Japan to continue their education.

The students were in a radical mood. They wanted to find the secret of Western power and success—the power that Japan had used to conquer Korea.[4] A former student during those turbulent years wrote that all they spoke of was liberty, independence, and Christianity.[5] In their desire to obtain the secret formula for the "second-hand" success of Japan, many were ready to reject large parts of their own cultural heritage. Yi Kwang-su, who two years later was active in the March First Movement, wrote that "the West

[2] San Kim and Nym Wales, *Song of Ariran*, p. 32; Younghill Kang, *The Grass Roof*, p. 242.

[3] Kang, *The Grass Roof*, p. 205. Students were attracted to Japan rather than to other nations during this period because of its proximity to Korea, the similarity of language, and the comparatively low cost owing to aid extended by some Japanese and the opportunity to obtain part-time employment. Before the Great Earthquake of September, 1923, China was ignored "because the level of culture in China was low" and there were few "jobs for educated Koreans available." Kim and Wales, *Song of Ariran*, p. 39.

[4] Kang, *The Grass Roof*, p. 253.

[5] *Ibid.*, p. 244; SP155, p. 66.

has developed a peculiar form of civilization and . . . this civilization is superior to that of the East."[6]

Most of the Korean students in Japan congregated in Tokyo where, in the relatively free atmosphere of student life, many became ardent advocates of Korean nationalism.[7] They formed societies for mutual aid, debate, and study of Japanese.[8] In an alien land, the Korean Y.M.C.A. in Kanda, a Tokyo district, provided them with a haven. The secretary, a Korean, welcomed the students, although most of them were non-Christians.[9] A former student wrote, "I saw a Korean Y.M.C.A. and because of the name, Korea, on the outside, I investigated."[10] The building soon became the unofficial headquarters for Korean student social activities and political meetings.

The great majority of the Korean students in Japan were self-supporting.[11] They delivered newspapers and milk, corrected proofs at publishing houses, worked in factories, and pulled jinrickshas.[12] Some of them went from door to door asking for old books, magazines, and clothing to sell. Often the poorer students would enter a restaurant and demand

[6] Yi Kwang-su, "What Christianity Has Done for Korea," *Missionary Review of the World*, Old Series, XLI (August, 1918), 607. Yi attended Waseda University and studied English literature. He was Korea's first "modern author" and was considered by many its best. Kim and Wales, *Song of Ariran*, p. 56.

[7] The Korean students in Tokyo were "scattered among all kinds of institutions, with no restrictions . . . on courses they might take." "The Korean Nationalist Movement," *Korea Review*, I (August, 1919), 15. Lee, "The Korean Nationalist Movement, 1905–1945," p. 279.

[8] Green, *The Christian Movement in Japan*, p. 159.

[9] *Ibid.*, p. 160.

[10] Kang, *The Grass Roof*, p. 251.

[11] It was generally the self-supporting students who were in trouble with the police for anti-Japanese activities.

[12] Kang, *The Grass Roof*, p. 237. Kim and Wales, *Song of Ariran*, pp. 32–34.

The March First Movement

that the more prosperous Korean students feed them. When desperate, the hungry students stole to eat.[13]

The Korean students' hatred of all Japanese was modified as they made friends with individuals. One student liked many of the Japanese he met in Japan and found that "all the Japanese housewives and girls were kind."[14] Another remarked that "everybody was polite and smiling to me. I began to lose my strong prejudices against the Japanese, and to see that they were like the Koreans — some good, some bad."[15]

The Growth of Nationalism Among the Students

During the Taisho period (1912–1926), Japan experienced a "great upsurge of liberalism,"[16] which developed into a movement supported mainly by liberal journalists and educators. University professors such as Yoshino Sakuzō and Minobe Tatsukichi explained how the democracy of the West could be adapted to the Japanese culture. These professors instilled liberal ideas in the minds of their students by means of lectures and discussion groups.[17]

The atmosphere of increasing liberalism in Japan permitted the Korean students to play an important role in the 1919 March First Movement which eventually brought about a modification of Japanese colonial rule in the peninsula. The nationalist sentiments of the Korean students found some support among Japanese professors and students. Professor Yoshino Sakuzō at Tokyo University, for example, encouraged them through personal contacts and

[13] Kim and Wales, *ibid.*, pp. 33–34.
[14] *Ibid.*
[15] Kang, *The Grass Roof*, p. 236.
[16] Ryusaku Tsunoda, et al., *Sources of the Japanese Tradition*, p. 724.
[17] *Ibid.*, p. 719.

through his published works.[18] Japanese members of the Shinjinkai (New Man's Society), a liberal discussion group established in December, 1918, by law students at Tokyo University, were openly in favor of Korean independence. This organization included both Japanese and Korean members.[19]

In 1916 there were seven Korean student organizations in Japan. Five were in Tokyo, one in Osaka, and one in Kyoto. All held political discussions, and some advocated the overthrow of the Japanese government in Korea. In 1920, as a result, 151 of the 212 Koreans on the police blacklist in Japan were students.[20]

Compared to their fellow students in Korea, however, the Korean students in Japan had a great deal of freedom. They published magazines attacking the Japanese annexation, and they circulated anti-Japanese propaganda received from Koreans in the United States, Hawaii, and China. At that time, Japanese laws concerning security and publication were much less strict in Japan than in Korea, so the Korean students were able to carry on their work openly.[21]

In March, 1909, the Taehan Hunghak-hoe (Greater Korean Promotion of Education Association) in Tokyo began to publish articles denouncing the contemplated annexation of Korea. After annexation, the Hagu-hoe (Student Fraternal Association) started publishing *Hak-chi-kwang* (Light of Study) in 1914. Of the nine issues published up to May, 1916, four were suppressed by the government because of their anti-Japanese content. Korean students also received and distributed 300 copies of Pak Un-sik's *Hanguk T'ongsa* (*Tragic History of Korea*), published in Shanghai.

[18] Lee, "The Korean Nationalist Movement, 1905–1945," p. 280.
[19] *Ibid.*, p. 281.
[20] *Ibid.*, pp. 279–280.
[21] *Ibid.*, pp. 281–282.

The March First Movement

Some of these student journals were smuggled into Korea. Three Korean students at Meiji University were arrested for writing anti-Japanese material which they intended to send abroad.[22]

Korean Students Provide the Spark

Yi Kwang-su, one of the most well-known student leaders of the period, became a leader of the March First Movement. His radical idealism epitomized the spirit of Korean nationalism. To a group of Korean students in Tokyo, Yi stressed the need for a stronger Korea.[23] In 1916, at a meeting of the Hagu-hoe in the Tokyo Korean Y.M.C.A., he forcefully opposed the migration of Japanese into Korea and urged that all Koreans should unite and fight.[24]

When the news of the First World War armistice reached Japan, the Korean students were greatly aroused by President Woodrow Wilson's pronouncements for self-determination. During December, 1918, and January, 1919, they "debated the problem of independence in radical tones, and asserted that one must sacrifice one's life for the cause of independence."[25] A committee of ten, elected to plan the details, decided to send a declaration of independence to the Japanese government and to foreign diplomatic missions in Japan.[26] One student was delegated to take a copy of the declaration and a message to the independence leaders in Korea.[27]

The plans and the declaration of the students in Japan

[22] *Ibid.*, p. 282.
[23] *Ibid.*
[24] *Ibid.*, p. 283.
[25] *Ibid.*, p. 296.
[26] *Ibid.*, pp. 296–297.
[27] *Ibid.*, p. 299.

encouraged the historian and publisher Ch'oe Nam-sŏn and other important Koreans on the peninsula to support the independence movement actively and openly.[28] Korean students were also profoundly influenced by these efforts of their counterparts in Japan. The two groups had frequent contacts. Those in Japan spent their summer vacations in Korea, traveling to every part of the country, teaching farmers to read and write, and spreading the nationalist doctrine along with grammar and writing lessons.[29] The plans of students in Japan to demonstrate for independence "highly aroused" the students in Korea, where the spark was ignited under the discontent on the peninsula.[30]

The Japanese police had noticed the word "Korea" preceding the title "Y.M.C.A." on the building in Kanda and observed that the Korean students were engaged in an unusual amount of activity. The police forced the students to discontinue several meetings and arrested some of their leaders. The students, however, continued to collect funds, print petitions, and reproduce the declaration of independence in English and Japanese as well as in Korean.[31] The police planned a raid of student boarding houses and the Y.M.C.A. for the morning of February 8, but the students anticipated their action and, that morning before police arrived, mailed the printed materials to members of the Japanese government, foreign diplomatic missions, and scholars.[32] That afternoon, two hundred students met at the Y.M.C.A. to discuss the independence movement. The police also attended and, when the discussion became heated, ordered the meeting closed. When the students refused to

[28] *Ibid.*, p. 302.
[29] *Ibid.*, p. 705.
[30] *Ibid.*, pp. 279, 301–302, 304.
[31] *Ibid.*, p. 300.
[32] *Ibid.*

obey, twenty-seven were arrested and nine later received prison sentences from seven to nine months.[33]

The petition submitted by the students was a strong indictment of Japanese rule in Korea. The Japanese were accused of breaking their written agreements, of "barbaric" and "treacherous" behavior in disregarding the interests of the Korean people, and of displaying "racial" arrogance. The petition demanded that Korea be freed from Japanese rule; it promised "an eternal war of blood upon the Japanese" if these demands went unheeded.[34]

On March 1, 1919, a declaration of independence was proclaimed in Seoul by Korean nationalist leaders. It was much more moderate in tone than the student document, but it was the beginning of the March First Movement. The signers of the declaration avoided threats and appealed to the moral sense of the Japanese.[35] The independence leaders had planned a series of peaceful demonstrations for that date throughout Korea, protesting Japanese actions in the peninsula and demanding independence. When the Japanese brutally suppressed the demonstrations, the movement turned into "a racial struggle against the Japanese as a whole."[36] From one to two million people took part in mass protests which lasted for two months. Japanese sources for the period from March 1 to April 30, 1919, set the number killed at 553, those injured at 1,409, and those arrested at 26,713. Korean nationalist sources, for a one year period following March 1, list 7,645 Koreans killed and 45,562 injured.[37] These demonstrations were different from earlier

[33] Yi Kwang-su was not among those arrested. He fled to Shanghai before February 8. *Ibid.*, pp. 300–301.
[34] For the petition see "Independence Movement in Japan," *Korea Review*, I (May, 1919), 84–85.
[35] Carlton W. Kendall, *The Truth about Korea*, p. 50.
[36] Lee, "The Korean Nationalist Movement, 1905–1945," p. 323.
[37] *Ibid.*, p. 324, and p. 114.

protests, such as the Tonghak Rebellion of 1894, in that Koreans of all classes took an active part and were united nationally against their common enemy.[38]

The massive demonstrations in Korea brought a quick response from the Japanese public. The government was forced to review its Korean policy. For the first time since annexation, the question of the Koreans and their place in the Japanese Empire was thrown open to public debate.

Reaction to the March First Movement

Many Japanese now seriously reconsidered Japan's position in Korea. Some suggested that Japan abandon her policy of forced assimilation; others advocated freedom for the Koreans. One Japanese scholar writing in the popular magazine *Taiyō* (Sun) in July, 1919, stated that the policy of assimilation had failed. He believed that the Japanese government had committed a grave error when it initiated the assimilation policy in 1910, and even more so "now that the spirit of democracy and the ideal of the self-determination of peoples is in so great [a] vogue throughout the world; to try to assimilate the Koreans in these circumstances would be as futile as an attempt at extinguishing a furious fire with an antiquated hand-pump." [39]

The activities of the Korean students in Japan and events in the peninsula also stimulated Japanese students to support Korean nationalism. In the summer of 1919, Professor Yoshino Sakuzō and groups of Japanese students began to meet more often with Korean and Chinese students to discuss mutual problems and to try to understand the customs

[38] Clarence N. Weems, Jr., "The Korean Reform and Independence Movement," p. 355.
[39] "Assimilation," *Korea Review*, II (August, 1920), 8–9.

The March First Movement

and attitudes of the Koreans and Chinese.[40] Yoshino felt that if the Korean issue "were submitted to the students, ninety in a hundred would say 'Give her independence or autonomy.' "[41]

Yanagi Sōetsu, who later founded the Museum of Japanese Folk Art in Tokyo, wrote a series of newspaper articles strongly criticizing Japan's policy of assimilation. He held Japan responsible for the March First Movement. "I appeal to the Korean people," Yanagi said, "to take note that some of us are now aware of our country's failure to follow the rightful way of humanity."[42]

In response to these and other protests, the Japanese government acted quickly and installed a new governor-general, Baron Saitō Makoto, on the peninsula. An imperial rescript in August, 1919, promised "fair and impartial treatment in all respects" and "certain reforms in the administrative organization of the Government-General."[43]

Saitō's administration proposed basic reforms which included "the establishment of nondiscrimination between Japanese and Koreans" and "a cultural policy" that would raise "the Korean people to the same standard as [that of] the Japanese."[44] These proposals and the imperial rescript admitted the existence of discrimination against Koreans, but, at the same time, suggested that the Japanese felt culturally superior to the Koreans. To implement the reform program, Saitō's administration permitted the revival of several Korean language newspapers, promised to respect Korean

[40] Sakuzō Yoshino, "Liberalism in Japan" in K. K. Kawakami (ed.), *What Japan Thinks*, pp. 89–90.
[41] *Ibid.*, p. 91.
[42] Naokichi Ubukata, "Nihonjin no Chōsen kan," *Shisō* (Thought), No. 448 (October, 1961), 1265.
[43] Michimasa Soyeshima, *Oriental Interpretations of the Far Eastern Problem*, p. 62.
[44] *Ibid.*, p. 61.

culture and customs, and pledged nondiscrimination between Japanese and Koreans in appointing government officials. In a directive issued to high officials on September 3, 1919, Saitō explained that the purpose of his administrative reforms was "to give [Koreans] more happiness and satisfaction than is the case at present by bringing their treatment socially and politically on the same footing as the Japanese. . . . The Koreans and the Japanese must be treated alike as members of the same family."[45]

In further efforts toward assimilation in this period, Saitō organized a public-information section to familiarize the Japanese and Korean peoples with each other's customs. Motion pictures about Japanese life were shown to Koreans in twenty different cities. People were encouraged to attend public lectures about Japan, and pamphlets were widely distributed.[46] The Japanese of the home islands were also subjected to a propaganda campaign about Korean life and customs. The government sponsored cinematographic exhibitions in Tokyo, Osaka, and Kyoto to introduce Korea to the general public in Japan. As in Korea, public lectures were given and pamphlets were distributed. This campaign seems to have met with little success. At a press convention in Seoul in May, 1923, Saitō noted that the Japanese were still unfamiliar with Korean conditions.[47]

Although the Japanese government was forced to grant concessions to the Koreans, its fundamental policy remained the same. Premier Hara Kei left no doubt of this when he stated in November, 1919, that Japan intended to assimilate the Koreans.[48] In July, 1920, the *Seoul Press*, the official

[45] Government-General of Chosen, *Annual Report on Administration of Chosen, 1922–23*, pp. 23, 227–228.
[46] *Ibid.*
[47] *Trans-Pacific*, May 19, 1923, p. 15.
[48] "Assimilation," *Korea Review*, II (August, 1920), 8–9.

The March First Movement

Japanese organ, published an editorial that made Japanese policy clear to any who might have missed Hara's remark: "We will not, however, waver in our determination to Japanize the Korean people, for we believe that our intention is right and just and that in Japanizing them we are promoting their welfare." [49]

After the failure of the March First Movement, the Korean students became more radical.[50] Twenty-one students who had studied in Japan, including student leader Yi Kwang-su, joined the new Korean Provisional Government established in Shanghai by Korean patriots in Siberia, Manchuria, China, and the United States.[51] Efforts were made by the provisional government to gain recognition at the Paris Peace Conference, the Washington Disarmament Conference, and at the League of Nations. Involved in these efforts was Syngman Rhee, a former student at Princeton under university president Woodrow Wilson. Rhee became head of a permanent Korean commission in Washington, D.C. Concerned by these new turns in Korean student patriotic activities and by the increased contact between Ko-

---

[49] Hugh Cynn, "A Korean View of Pacific Relations," Institute of Pacific Relations, Honolulu Session, June 30–July 14, 1925, p. 81.
[50] Kim and Wales, *Song of Ariran*, p. 30.
[51] Lee, "The Korean Nationalist Movement, 1905–1945," p. 279. The Korean Provisional Government was established by exile leaders in the French Concession in Shanghai in 1919. There were other groups of exiles in Manchuria, Siberia, and the United States. From 1919 until 1921 the provisional government in Shanghai and the other exile groups worked closely together. In 1921, however, after Syngman Rhee, who had been elected premier of the Korean Provisional Government on April 10, 1919, arrived in Shanghai the exile movement was torn apart by factionalism. From 1921 to 1930 the provisional government was weak, but it continued to worry the Japanese government because of the terrorists it sometimes sent to Japan and Korea. The Koreans in Japan sometimes cooperated with the Shanghai provisional government, but it did not have direct control of their organizations.

reans and sympathetic Japanese students, Japanese police stepped up their surveillance of Korean activities on the islands.

Although the Japanese government and public probably did not fully understand the part that Korean students in Japan played in the March First Movement or the strength of their nationalism, developments in 1919 did leave the Japanese authorities with a deeper impression that Koreans in Japan were subversive and were not to be trusted. The Japanese press often carried derogatory and distorted or false stories about Koreans.[52] Japanese suspicions were further increased by rumors of Korean plots to kill the Emperor and his officials. When Premier Hara was assassinated by a Japanese on November 4, 1921, the rumor spread that he had been killed by a Korean.[53] These events further estranged the peoples of the two countries just at the time when large numbers of Korean laborers began entering Japan in search of work and a higher standard of living.

[52] Harry Emerson Wildes, *Social Currents in Japan*, pp. 293–295.
[53] "Assassination of Hara," *Korea Review*, III (November, 1921), 16.

III
ORIGINS OF THE KOREAN MINORITY PROBLEM, 1920–1930

Traditionally, Korean farmers have a close attachment to their birthplace and to the grave mounds that occupy the slopes around their villages. The Japanese annexation of Korea, however, disrupted the traditional pattern of rural life and eventually led to the migration of millions of Koreans, some to Manchuria, Outer Mongolia, and Siberia, and some through the narrow Tsushima Strait seeking seasonal employment in the industrial and mining areas of Japan.

The Immigration of Korean Laborers

After Japanese annexation, farm tenancy rose rapidly and a large landless class developed in Korea. Before 1910 all land was owned by the sovereign, but farmers had recognized cultivation rights if they paid the tax and fulfilled other obligations. The Japanese government, in an effort to modernize the Korean economy and in order to fix landownership, carried out an extensive land survey between 1910 and 1918. Farmers were instructed to register their land within a specified period, but many of the illiterate farmers did not understand the procedure and lost title to their land. The Yangban (local gentry) enriched themselves during this period of confusion by filing claims to public lands and even to the lands of independent farmers. The increase in the use of money and a new tax structure caused other farmers to fall into debt.[1]

Between 1915 and 1930, the population of Korea increased 30 per cent, but the number of new jobs failed to rise as rapidly. The increase in population, combined with the rapid development of a landless class, imposed great economic hardship on the Korean people.[2] A Japanese government report of 1925 listed the following reasons for the migration of hundreds of thousands of Koreans to Japan: bad economic conditions in Korea because of bad weather and poor crops, the hope of higher pay for labor in Japan, and encouragement from countrymen who had returned to Korea from the islands.[3]

The majority, perhaps even 90 per cent, of the Koreans who went to Japan had been tenant farmers or unskilled laborers[4] from the rice-growing areas of southern Korea.[5]

[1] Chong-sik Lee, *The Politics of Korean Nationalism*, pp. 11, 14, 93–94. Also see Andrew J. Grajdanzev, *Modern Korea*, p. 110.
[2] Irene B. Taeuber, "The Population Potential of Postwar Korea," *The Far Eastern Quarterly*, V (May, 1946), 298–299.
[3] SP155, p. 25.
[4] Ryoichi Ishii, *Population Pressure and Economic Life in Japan*, p. 207. Naimushō Keihokyoku, *Shōwa hachinen-chū ni okeru shakai undō no jōkyō*, 1933, p. 1397. Hereafter cited as SUJ with appropriate date. This publication, marked "highly secret," was published annually from 1929 to 1942.
[5] Irene B. Taeuber, *The Population of Japan*, p. 189.

The new arrivals usually journeyed to urban centers where they could find other Koreans to aid them while they looked for work. Few migrants had specific jobs waiting for them in Japan. Without special skills, they became jiyūrōdōsha (casual laborers) or hiyatoininpu (daily workers).[6]

The Japan to which the Koreans migrated was beset with economic problems. The First World War had stimulated the Japanese economy to expand at a hurried rate, and the number of factories and workers increased greatly. The war years were characterized by an expanding economy that eagerly absorbed the cheap Korean labor flowing into Japan. "In contrast, the years from the depression of 1920 through that of 1929 and down to the Manchurian Incident in 1931 were marked by depressed economic conditions and large scale unemployment."[7] By 1931 the number of jobless workers in Japan had reached 3,000,000.[8] The desperation of Japanese labor was reflected in the increasing number of strikes during the 1920's to demand higher wages or to protest wage reductions.[9]

During this period of acute economic depression, the influx of Korean laborers into Japan increased rapidly. In 1921, there were 39,000 Koreans in Japan, but in 1930 the number had increased to approximately 400,000.[10] Since many Japanese were unemployed, competition for jobs was keen. It was especially difficult to find work in Tokyo, Osaka, and the other large cities — the very places to which most Koreans migrated. The Koreans were often forced to take

[6] SUJ, 1933, p. 1397. The jiyūrōdōsha might hold the same job for several weeks or even months. The hiyatoininpu held a different job each day.
[7] Kazuo Okochi, *Labor in Modern Japan*, p. 56.
[8] *Ibid.*, p. 61.
[9] Shuichi Harada, *Labor Conditions in Japan*, pp. 176–177.
[10] SP155, p. 23; Ishii, *Population Pressure and Economic Life in Japan*, p. 207.

low-paying jobs or undesirable work. In 1925, most of the immigrants were employed as laborers, coal miners, or road repairmen. Very few were factory workers.[11] Even the acceptance of low wages and miserable living conditions failed to keep all the Koreans employed and more than 20,000 were without work in 1925.[12]

In that year, the Koreans in Japan included approximately 106,000 laborers, 2,600 students, and 200 intellectuals,[13] scattered throughout Japan from Hokkaido in the north to Okinawa in the south.[14] Osaka had the largest concentration with 34,311, and Tokyo, with 9,989, ranked third.[15] Only 21,450 of the Korean immigrants were women.[16]

Illiteracy, a high crime rate, and a lack of permanency characterized the group of unskilled Korean laborers.[17] Among 18,191 Koreans in Osaka who were investigated by the city government in April, 1922, more than 54 per cent were illiterate in both Japanese and Korean, only 15 per cent were able to understand Japanese, and about thirty-

[11] *Ibid.*, p. 7.
[12] R. A. Hardie, "Koreans in Japan," *The Korean Mission Field*, XXI (June, 1925), 121.
[13] SP155, p. 27. Under the new "cultural policy" Korean students were given more encouragement to study in Japan. The number of students in Japan increased rapidly, and then, after the earthquake of September, 1923, decreased just as rapidly. Some returned home and vowed never to study in Japan again. As a security measure the government temporarily halted immigration from Korea, and no new students were admitted for some months. But in 1925 the number of students studying in Japan jumped to a total of 2,656. Two-thirds of them were under junior high-school age and only 81 were attending a university. Most students were studying in Tokyo (1,322), Kyoto (180), and Osaka (127). SP155, pp. 31–32, 213–214. See also *Annual Report on Administration of Chosen, 1926–27*, pp. 99.
[14] SP155, p. 29.
[15] *Ibid.*, pp. 27–28.
[16] *Ibid.*, p. 22.
[17] *Ibid.*, p. 25.

Origins of the Minority Problems

one per cent understood the language slightly.[18] A decade later, in a 1933 report compiled by the Japanese Home Ministry, it was noted that most Korean laborers still did not understand Japanese and could neither read nor write the language.[19]

Many Koreans planned to work in Japan only long enough to save some money, others came just for the winter relief projects, and many returned to Korea each New Year's Day. Between 1924 and 1928, more than 200,000 Koreans crossed the Korea Strait each year going to and from Japan.[20]

While in the islands, Koreans often lived in wretched conditions and few had their own homes. Usually, they occupied quarters provided by the factory in which they worked or in buildings owned by Korean landlords.[21] The poorest were crowded with as many as ten people who shared a six-tatami room. Others built shacks or put up tents.[22]

According to official Japanese documents, the Koreans were "lazy," used their extra money for gambling and sake, and made no effort to improve themselves.[23] Missionary reports confirm the miserable living conditions and the fondness for intoxicants. The Reverend R. A. Hardie wrote,

---

[18] *Ibid.*

[19] SUJ, 1933, p. 1397.

[20] Ishii, *Population Pressure and Economic Life in Japan*, pp. 207–208. Around 1925 the Japanese government enacted laws for the relief of unemployed laborers. Since many Korean laborers fell into this class a seasonal migration developed. By 1929 the majority of laborers engaged in the "winter unemployment relief public works" were Korean.

[21] SP155, p. 42.

[22] *Ibid.*, p. 43. A *tatami* is a floor mat, about six by three feet, woven from rice straw. A six-*tatami* room would be about nine by twelve feet.

[23] *Ibid.*, pp. 5, 44. SUJ, 1933, p. 1397.

In the larger cities they congregate in tenement houses . . . with little provision for sanitation. I saw one two-story tenement house, divided into sixty rooms, each nine feet square, occupied by 500 men, women, and children, many of them without work. . . . They are allowed off work two days in the month when they purchase "sake" by the tub, and gather in large groups to feast and drink, often terminating the day by a general fight in which it is said men are sometimes killed.[24]

Relations Between the Immigrants and the Japanese

To migrants from the Korean countryside, the noise and confusion of Osaka and Tokyo must have ben perplexing. The new arrivals had to adjust to the culture of the city in an alien country, using only the few phrases they knew of a strange language. It is not surprising that illiterate Korean farmboys living a squalid existence in dirty Japanese industrial cities should have had a higher crime rate than the Japanese,[25] or that conflict arose between the newly arrived Korean farmers and the Japanese farmers who had also just left their countryside to live in the cities. Both of these highly mobile groups from conservative backgrounds competed for the limited number of positions open to unskilled laborers in the Japanese industrial complexes. The Japanese farmers "brought the heritage of physical poverty, the conservatism of feudal times, and the narrowness of an intellectually limited milieu into the greatest of cities." [26]

This double infusion of labor resulted in a sudden upsurge in the populations of metropolitan industrial areas

---

[24] Hardie, "Koreans in Japan," pp. 121–122.
[25] SUJ, 1933, p. 1644.
[26] Irene B. Taeuber, "Population and Labor Force in the Industrialization of Japan, 1850–1950" in Simon S. Kuznets (ed.), *Economic Growth*, p. 355. Most of the Japanese laborers came from agrarian regions. *Ibid.*, p. 336.

Origins of the Minority Problems 33

and in a critical housing shortage, especially in Osaka, where disputes between Korean tenants and Japanese landlords were the most serious. By 1925, disagreement over rented houses had become a "racial problem"[27] in Tokyo and Kanagawa[28] as well as in Osaka. Most disputes arose because the Koreans did not have the money to pay the rent; some were in arrears for as long as a year.

The Japanese complained that the Koreans were noisy and did not take care of the rented houses in which they lived. Because of these problems, many landlords refused to rent to Koreans. Koreans, in turn, resented the landlords' attitudes.[29] These tensions also affected the student population. A former Korean student in Japan during the 1920's wrote that the Japanese disliked renting rooms to self-supporting students because they refused to pay the rent and moved out if the landlord asked for the money.[30]

In the depressed economy of Japan, these misunderstandings between landlord and tenant were aggravated by the mutual dislike of Japanese and Koreans. A Japanese government report elaborated on the attitude of the Japanese toward the Koreans: "In custom, Koreans are basically different from Japanese; and their general life is very unclean and unplanned. Thus, it is natural that the Japanese do not like to live close to them. They are very strange and get very jealous and misunderstand things. There is a tendency for Japanese to look at them with contempt."[31]

A Christian missionary, writing about the Koreans in Japan, pointed out that many Koreans who migrated to Japan were "not Korea's best" and that in Japan, they "shed those mild dispositions which make them so friendly and

[27] SP155, p. 174.
[28] *Ibid.*, p. 173.
[29] *Ibid.*, p. 182.
[30] San Kin and Nym Wales, *Song of Ariran*, p. 34.
[31] SP155, p. 173.

lovable in Korea" and became "almost truculent." "In many places the house owners refuse to rent them houses at any price; if Koreans move in, the Japanese house renters nearby will begin to try to move out." [32]

In addition to disputes over housing, the number of disagreements between Japanese and Koreans rose rapidly after 1922 and reached its highest point just after the Great Kantō Earthquake of September 1, 1923.[33] The incidents usually involved "very low class" Koreans, and, during 1925 none of the intelligentsia. The two main causes for the incidents were ethnic differences and drunkenness. Since the Japanese regarded them as "inferior people" (rettō minzoku), Koreans always had a feeling of being "different." [34]

Despite racial prejudice and friction, there were many examples of cooperation, friendship, and even intermarriage.[35] Members of the more radical Korean organizations made contacts with Japanese extremists. The Kokutokai (Black Wave Association), for example, cooperated with Japanese anarchists. When the police seized the members of the Kokutokai, they arrested twelve Koreans and five Japanese. Pak Yŏl (Boku Retsu), the leader, had a Japanese common-law wife.[36] The Ichigatsukai (January Society)

[32] C. A. Clark, "The Korean Church in Japan," *The Japan Christian Quarterly*, VII (July, 1932), 264.
[33] SP155, p. 174. January–September, 1922 (9 months), 75 incidents; January–October, 1923 (10 months), 227 incidents; entire year of 1924, 48 incidents; January to October of 1925, 116 incidents.
[34] *Ibid.*, pp. 175–176.
[35] Eisuke Yoshio, "Chōsenjin no naichi tokō," *Gaikō Jiho*, LIII (March 15, 1930), 175. At the end of 1927 there were 499 mixed marriages of Koreans and Japanese. The number seems to apply only to those living in Japan.
[36] SP155, pp. 74–75. Pak Yŏl, aged twenty-one, the central figure among the Korean anarchists in Japan, was on good terms with such Japanese anarchists as Ōsugi Sakae and Iwasa Sakutarō. In November, 1921, Pak and several other Koreans organized the Kokutokai. Pak acted as its head, but the association was controlled by Ōsugi and other

had Japanese members and was in close contact with leftwing Japanese associations.[37] Japanese students attended the meetings of the Shinseikai (New Star Society)[38] and the Sanichi Musan Seinenkai (March First Proletarian Youth Association) of Osaka, both of which cooperated with leftwing Japanese.[39] Organized Japanese and Korea labor tended to support each other against their common enemy, capitalism, but the majority of laborers in Japan were not organized. As early as August, 1919, the Dai Nippon Rōdōkumiai Sōdōmei Yūaikai (Grand Japan Federation of Labor Unions Fraternal Association) adopted a resolution declaring "equal treatment for Japanese and foreign workers."[40] In May, 1927, the Nippon Rōdō Hyōgikai (Japan Labor Union Council) advocated "aid for the labor movements in Korea and Formosa."[41] The Rōdō Nōmintō (Labor-Farmer Party) called for the "abolition of discrimination against the subject races."[42] Other labor groups voiced similar sentiments.[43]

Korean organized labor was continually in close contact Japanese anarchists. The Kokutokai was formed specifically to draw Koreans into the ranks of the Japanese anarchists. Just before the catastrophic earthquake of September, 1923, the Japanese police arrested Pak and his wife, Kaneko Ayako, on a charge of having attempted to purchase bombs. The police, however, later charged them with plotting to kill the Emperor and his son. On March 23, 1926, they were sentenced to death, but the sentence was later commuted to life imprisonment. Pak was released in 1945. His wife had died a few months after they were sentenced. SUJ, 1932, p. 1517. See also Kyoto daigaku bungakubu kokushi kenkyūshitsu hen, *Nihon kindaishi jiten*, p. 560.
[37] SP155, p. 80.
[38] *Ibid.*, p. 91.
[39] *Ibid.*, p. 95.
[40] Okochi, *Labor in Modern Japan*, p. 43.
[41] Harada, *Labor Conditions in Japan*, p. 202.
[42] *Ibid.*, p. 208.
[43] *Ibid.*, p. 214.

with its Japanese counterparts. The Chōsen Musansha Shakai Renmei (Korean Proletarian Social League), organized in Osaka on June 28, 1924, was active in establishing a protective association for Korean factory workers. Members of the group sometimes attended meetings of the Nihon Rōdō Sōdōmei Osaka Rengō (Allied Japan Labor Federation in Osaka) and the Zenkoku Suiheisha (National Leveling League), both of which were demanding social equality and were, therefore, natural allies of the suppressed Koreans. In August, 1924, these Japanese groups helped the Korean Proletarian League organize a labor meeting.[44]

The Zainihon Chōsen Rōdō Sōdōmei (Federation of Labor of the Koreans in Japan), organized in February 1925, had its headquarters in Tokyo. The Koreans imitated the structure and principles of the Nihon Rōdō Sōdōmei (Japanese Federation of Labor) when they created the Korean federation. The Korean group hoped to enlist all the Korean laborers in Japan and then to extend the organization to the peninsula. In March, leaders of the Korean labor group in Japan attended a nationwide meeting of the Nihon Rōdō Sōdōmei, and explained that their purpose in forming a Korean labor federation had nothing to do with racial discrimination against the Japanese, and that they hoped to join forces with the Japanese Federation of Labor.[45]

In 1924 at the annual Tokyo May Day demonstration of the Japanese Federation of Labor, thirty members of the Kokudokai (National Society), a Korean group, joined the march. Two Koreans managed to give brief speeches and were applauded by the Japanese marchers before the police stopped them.[46] The following year, Japanese labor unions

[44] SP155, pp. 96–97. The National Leveling League was formed in March, 1922, by members of the former pariah class (Eta).
[45] Ibid., pp. 98–107.
[46] Ibid., p. 114.

in Osaka invited the Koreans to attend the planning meeting and to take part in the May Day demonstration and march. The Koreans accepted because it was their "only chance to stand in the same line with Japanese labor and show their power."[47]

Government reports list many other instances of cooperation between Japanese and Korean organized labor, but the number of Koreans who actually participated was small. Only 370 of the 34,311 Koreans in Osaka attended the 1925 May Day demonstration in that city, although many groups tried to get Koreans to join.[48] Most Korean laborers in Japan were not interested in joining labor organizations or taking part in demonstrations.

"Peace and friendship associations" were gradually established throughout Japan, initially by Korean and Japanese intellectuals who sought to encourage peaceful contacts between the two peoples. The new groups were created to oppose the many anti-Japanese organizations that were spreading "dangerous thoughts" in Japan.[49] The Sōaikai (Mutual Love Society) was launched in Osaka in 1923.[50] In 1925 the membership was reported at 35,000, and there were branches in Nagoya, Kyoto, Kobe, Yokohama, Tokyo, Hokkaido, Kyushu, and even Karafuto (Sakhalin). A branch office in Pusan, Korea, handled prospective immigrants to the mainland of Japan. Very early, perhaps even before its formal organization, the Sōaikai received financial backing from the Osaka city government.[51] During the 1930's, the central Japanese government increasingly regarded it as a tool for controlling the Korean minority. The

[47] *Ibid.*, pp. 119–121.
[48] *Ibid.*, pp. 27, 123.
[49] SUJ, 1933, p. 1399.
[50] *Nihon kindaishi jiten*, p. 432.
[51] *Trans-Pacific*, October 25, 1924, p. 13.

name was changed to Kyōwa Jigyō (Concordia Enterprise) and, with a gift of 50,000 yen, the organization became subject to the authority of the Home Ministry in 1936.[52]

The number of Koreans belonging to the "friendship associations" is deceptive because membership was often a requirement for obtaining permission from the government to travel from Korea to Japan.[53] A Korean official of the Japan-Korea Friendship Association expressed a common Korean view when he declared that "more than 90 per cent of the public of Japan had deep-rooted prejudice against Koreans."[54]

The Great Kantō Earthquake

On September 1, 1923, at 11:58 A.M., the populous Kantō plain was struck by the most destructive earthquake ever recorded in Japan. The Kantō Dai Shinsai (the Great Kantō Earthquake) caused the death of about 100,000 people. The city of Tokyo was almost completely gutted by the vast fires that started after the earthquake. In addition, this catastrophe led to the massacre of several thousand Koreans.[55]

The outburst of racial hatred that developed into this mass murder had many causes. Prejudice against Koreans already had a long history in Japan. The influx of Korean labor, together with the events of 1919, intensified this feel-

[52] *Nihon kindaishi jiten*, p. 432.
[53] This was especially true after Japan entered the Second World War.
[54] *Trans-Pacific*, October 25, 1924, p. 13.
[55] *Sekai daihyakka jiten*, VI (1957), 456. Matsuo Takayoshi, a Japanese scholar who has done a thorough job of research on this incident, estimates that the jikeidan (vigilante corps) alone killed more than 2,000 Koreans. He also notes that a few Chinese and Japanese were slain by mistake. Takayoshi Matsuo, "Kantō daishinsai moto no Chōsenjin gyakusatsu jiken," *Shisō* (Thought), Part I, No. 471 (September, 1963), 54.

ing. Soon after the earthquake, rumors began to circulate that the Koreans were planning to attack the Japanese and were setting fires, looting, and poisoning wells. In the midst of the confusion that followed the earthquake, many Japanese believed these rumors. The Tokyo police made matters worse by authorizing a radio broadcast warning that the Koreans, aided by Japanese anarchists, "were burning houses, killing people, and stealing money and property."[56] Japanese army reservists and civilian volunteers were organized as vigilante corps to roam the streets in search of Koreans.

The charges against the Koreans were falsehoods.[57] The despised Koreans had become convenient scapegoats for the earthquake-stunned Japanese. The government was slow to act in this period of unprecedented crisis, perhaps because it was in the midst of a cabinet change, and nothing was done to calm public hysteria or to refute the rumors about marauding Koreans.

An official report in the *Japan Yearbook* lent credence to the earthquake rumors and helped perpetuate them.

The Korean scare in the downtown quarter of Tokyo at Honjo and other places originated from the isolated malpractices perpetrated in the hour of confusion following the shock and fire

[56] Kim and Wales, *Song of Ariran*, p. 37. Harry E. Wildes, "Japan's Struggle for Democracy," *The World Tomorrow*, VIII (June, 1925), 174–176. Two days after the earthquake the Home Ministry sent a telegram to subordinate governmental units in various parts of Japan. The telegram stated that during the earthquake-wrought confusion the Koreans had started fires and carried bombs which were part of a Korean plot. The local authorities were instructed to take strong measures to prevent any Korean subversion in their administrative areas. Matsuo, "Kantō daishinsai . . . ," p. 36.

[57] A report compiled by the police division of the Home Ministry clearly stated that the rumors about the Koreans were false. SP155, p. 175.

by a number of disorderly Koreans. About fifty criminal acts by Koreans were reported in Tokyo and properly dealt with. One case that occurred early in the morning of the third day near the only remaining water tap in the Kikugawa-Cho, Honjo, is significant. A suspicious-looking Korean in Japanese dress was noticed loitering near by [sic]. He was seized and examined by the refugees when a paper wrapper containing about an ounce of a whitish powder was discovered about his person. The man insisted it was common salt. He was forced to swallow it and soon died in agony. The powder was arsenic.[58]

The Japanese press continued to print unsubstantiated rumors about the Koreans, and this irresponsible attitude helped prolong the panic after the earthquake.[59]

During the disorder following the earthquake, the Japanese army and police indiscriminately murdered a number of Japanese radicals, including Hirasawa Keichi, a socialist, and eight other men who were butchered in their jail cells by soldiers because they sang revolutionary songs and used "improper language."[60] The anarchist Ōsugi Sakae, his wife, and a young nephew were also brutally murdered by the police.[61] On the other hand, the Japanese police were lax in apprehending those Japanese who had killed several thousand Koreans in the post-earthquake panic. When caught, the offenders were either released or given very light sentences of a year or a year-and-a-half in jail.[62]

By 1924, however, the Japanese realized the significance of events following the earthquake and began to react against their own excesses. Writing in a government report

[58] "The Earthquake and the Public Order," *The Japan Yearbook, 1924–25*, p. 241.
[59] Harry Emerson Wildes, *Social Currents in Japan*, p. 293.
[60] "The Earthquake and the Public Order," p. 243.
[61] Robert A. Scalapino, *Democracy and the Party Movement in Prewar Japan*, p. 326.
[62] Wildes, "Japan's Struggle for Democracy," p. 176.

approximately two years after the earthquake, a Japanese official maintained that the public had learned a lesson from the rash acts against Koreans in September, 1923, and were now inclined to treat Koreans better. He noted that the number of incidents between the two peoples had dropped sharply to only 48 during 1924. He might also have pointed out that the return of 40,000 Koreans to their homeland after the earthquake reduced the number of those with whom the Japanese could quarrel. Japanese remorse was short-lived, however, and conflicts between Japanese and Koreans started increasing again in 1925.[63] When asked about the Great Kantō Earthquake of 1923, educated Japanese, even today, still maintain that Koreans poisoned wells and attempted to kill the people of the islands.

Immigration Policy Toward the Koreans

The Japanese home government had no long-range plan for Korean immigration until the 1930's. Immigration policy had been determined during earlier decades on a pragmatic basis as each new situation arose. Government and newspaper reports and articles by scholars indicate that the Japanese were divided on the Korean immigration problem. Restrictive laws were not fully enforced. The total number of Korean immigrants in Japan rose from 3,630 in 1914 to 419,000 in 1930, a year of high unemployment rates and severe depression when the Japanese government was trying desperately to export surplus Japanese labor overseas.[64] Obviously, there were serious contradictions in Japan's immigration policy for Koreans.

---

[63] SP155, pp. 6, 176. From New Year's Day until October, the police recorded 116 conflicts.

[64] *Trans-Pacific*, August 8, 1929, p. 11. Kazuichiro Ono, "The Problem of Japanese Emigration," *Kyoto University Economic Review*, XXVIII (April, 1958), 47.

Before 1910, Chinese and Korean laborers could easily be prevented from entering Japan. A law of January 24, 1874, gave prefectural governors the right to refuse the landing of aliens for a variety of reasons.[65] After extra-territoriality had been abolished, Imperial Ordinance 352 of July 28, 1899, gave Chinese and Koreans the same privileges of residence in Japan as other aliens. They were allowed to move freely within the former foreign settlements, but, to reside outside, they needed special permission from local officials.[66] This pattern of local control of immigration continued. For Koreans, the Imperial Ordinance became invalid at the time of annexation in 1910.[67] Japan's annexation of Korea gave quasi-Japanese citizenship to the Koreans; the Japanese government could hardly legislate against the group it planned to assimilate. After 1910, the central government was caught in a dilemma between the demands of its new subjects and those of the Japanese home islands. This problem was further complicated by the alien exclusion laws enacted by the United States and Canada in 1923 and 1924.

The Japanese governor-general in Seoul did not always agree with the home government on how the peninsula should be administered. These differences were accentuated by the home government's ambivalence on the Korean immigration problem. After Saitō Makoto took office as governor-general in August, 1919, rule by the sword was changed to control of Korea by a cultural policy. In 1921 at a time when Japan was in the midst of an acute economic crisis with the rate of unemployment increasing daily, Saitō relaxed the restrictions on immigration of Koreans from

[65] Kiyo S. Inui, *The Unsolved Problem of the Pacific*, pp. 330–331.
[66] K. K. Kawakami, "Japan's Policy toward Alien Immigration," *Current History*, XX (June, 1924), 473.
[67] *Ibid.* Ono, "The Problem of Japanese Emigration," p. 46.

Origins of the Minority Problems 43

the peninsula to the home islands.[68] In June, 1923, he declared in a press statement that it would be "unreasonable" to exclude Koreans from Japanese industries just because they accepted lower wages than the Japanese.[69]

Japanese industry agreed with Saitō. Even during the depression of the 1920's, Japanese industrialists continued to demand cheap Korean labor[70] for which they sent labor agents to Korea.[71] Considering the close ties between government and business during the 1920's, the government may have hesitated to enact laws that would seriously impede this flow of labor and incur the wrath of industry.

Organized labor, which consisted of only 5 per cent of the working force, also put little pressure on the government to exclude Korean workers. Organized labor, which was urging equal treatment and pay for Koreans, could hardly have advocated their exclusion at this time.

Some Japanese scholars and journalists pointed out that all Koreans had a legal right to settle in Japan.[72] Early in 1923, the *Kokumin* advocated that Korean laborers "be imported, properly trained, and employed."[73] The *JiJi Shinpō*, while admitting that Korean labor might "constitute

---

[68] SP155, p. 26.

[69] *Trans-Pacific*, June 16, 1923, p. 4. There were many conflicts of interest between Seoul and Tokyo. See Harold S. Quigley, *Japanese Government and Politics*, pp. 315–316.

[70] *Trans-Pacific*, August 8, 1929, p. 11.

[71] Shunzo Yoshisaka, "Labour Recruiting in Japan and Its Control," *International Labour Review*, XII (July, 1925), 488.

[72] Michimasa Soyeshima, *Oriental Interpretations of the Far Eastern Problem*, p. 63. Like the government officials, scholars were divided in their attitudes toward Korean immigrants. Some opposed all emigration because it meant loss of manpower, and encouraged the government to invite immigrants to come to Japan. Others argued that Japan should export her surplus population and exclude immigrants. Ono, "The Problem of Japanese Emigration," p. 46.

[73] "Overpopulation and Immigration in Japan," *The Living Age*, CCCXVI (February 10, 1923), 315.

a serious menace to Japanese labor," said there was "no strong reason why it should be prevented" from immigrating to Japan.[74] The *Osaka Mainichi* regarded the rapid influx of Koreans as the cause of acute unemployment in Japan. But the same newspaper also said, "There is no means of preventing them from finding work in the homeland. This is beyond control."[75]

In October, 1925, despite support for Korean immigration, the government placed restrictions on Koreans entering Japan. Only the following were allowed to immigrate: those certain of securing employment, those who possessed sixty yen after all travel and employment fees were paid, those who were not under obligation to labor brokers in Korea, and those who had permits from their chief of police. Morphine addicts were excluded.[76]

The Katō Kōmei Ministry (June, 1924–August, 1925) of the Kenseikai (Constitutional Party) was in power when these restrictions were imposed. Just a month earlier the Kenseikai had been criticized in the press for suggesting that Koreans should be "encouraged to emigrate to Manchuria and Siberia to make room for Japanese in their own homeland."[77] This was the first time that such a policy had been openly advocated.

The restrictions of October, 1925, were only a limited deterrent to Korean immigration. In 1927, 83,477 Koreans were prevented from crossing the straits, but 246,809 were successful.[78] The government then stiffened the restrictions

[74] *Trans-Pacific*, August 11, 1923, p. 8.
[75] *Ibid.*, August 22, 1929, p. 8. At other times the press advocated the restriction of Korean immigration to solve the unemployment problem. Edward W. Wagner, *The Korean Minority in Japan, 1904–1950*, p. 23.
[76] Kamekichi Takahashi, *Nihon sangyō rōdō ron* (A study of Japan's industrial labor), pp. 448–449.
[77] *Trans-Pacific*, September 19, 1925, p. 3.
[78] Takahashi, *Nihon sangyō rōdō ron*, p. 448.

of October, 1925, by requiring that Koreans have jobs in Japan before leaving the peninsula, and that they understand Japanese. The amount of money required, however, was reduced to ten yen. In addition, the Home Ministry told Japanese businessmen that they might bring in only a specified number of Korean laborers.[79] This modified law was as ineffectual as the earlier one, and the number of new Korean arrivals to Japan continued to climb.[80] Evidently the restrictions were not fully enforced.

At times, government ambivalence toward the problem of Korean immigration took the form of indirectly encouraging unskilled Korean labor to come to Japan. During the 1920's, the central government, and later the provincial and city governments, promoted a plan for subsidized public works to help unskilled labor. But since no plan for such relief work was inaugurated for Korea, the *Osaka Mainichi* pointed out in 1925 that the plan would "inevitably encourage Korean coolies to come over to this country. It can be predicted . . . that Japan will encounter unpleasant experiences in this connection."[81] Because of the public works program, a seasonal migration developed with Koreans coming each year to register for work in the large cities of Japan. In 1929, the *Osaka Mainichi*, again criticizing government immigration policy, noted that "the total number of laborers employed in accordance with unemployment relief for the winter of 1928 was computed at 34,388, of which 18,675 were Koreans. This is 52.2 per cent."[82]

[79] SUJ, 1933, p. 1446.
[80] *Ibid.*, pp. 1440–1442. Ishii, *Population Pressure and Economic Life in Japan*, p. 207.
[81] *Trans-Pacific*, September 12, 1925, p. 8.
[82] *Ibid.*, August 22, 1929, p. 8. For a table that gives the proportion of Koreans among casual laborers between 1925 and 1928 see Seishi Idei, "The Unemployment Problem in Japan," *International Labour Review*, XXII (October, 1930), 510.

There were indeed reasons why the Japanese government might want to exclude Korean immigrants. The government-general, however, refused to do so. Japanese industry continued to demand cheap labor, and there was sympathy for the Koreans expressed in press and political opposition to the policy of assimilation. Perhaps another major reason no exclusion laws were forced on Koreans was that the Japanese remembered their own severe condemnation of such laws in the United States and Canada.

In his *Studies in Social Pathology*, Dr. Matoda Sakunoshin declared that "cheap Chinese and Korean labor cannot be excluded if we argue that Japanese workers must have the same right [of immigration to] the countries which exclude Asiatics."[83] The *JiJi Shinpō* wrote, "To deny them such treatment would be to commit a greater offense than the Californians are perpetrating against Japanese residents."[84]

Regardless of such moralizing, the Japanese government gradually tightened its control over Korean immigration. The restrictions discriminated against Koreans but, in practice, were loosely enforced.

The huge influx of Korean labor into Japan was not the cause of unemployment during the 1920's and early 1930's but only aggravated a situation which already existed. Japan as a rapidly industrializing nation, had begun to feel the effects of unemployment as early as 1905.[85] The relief and immigration policies of the government did little to solve either the problems of unemployment or of the Korean immigration.

Although the increasing number of disputes between Koreans and Japanese indicated their deteriorating rela-

---

[83] *Trans-Pacific*, May 12, 1923, p. 5.
[84] *Ibid.*, August 11, 1923, p. 8.
[85] *The Japan Yearbook, 1917*, p. 300.

Origins of the Minority Problems 47

tionship,[86] and barriers of language and customs still caused misunderstandings, nevertheless, the Koreans in Japan had made some gains during the 1920's. They could vote in Japanese elections,[87] and during the early 1930's a number became active in politics as candidates for public office. Most Koreans, though, did not fully participate in the life of Japanese communities, where they were still regarded as not wholly acceptable. For their part, Koreans did not seem eager to become full members of Japanese community life.

The government was aware of these problems. A report stated, "Generally, Koreans live in the slum section of a large city or they live in temporary quarters next to the place where they are working. The main reason . . . is that their language, manners, customs, and general way of life are different from those of the Japanese."[88]

---

[86] In 1925 there were only 27 rented housing disputes, but by 1933 there were 5,504. In 1933 there were approximately three and a half times more Koreans in Japan than in 1925; so a proportional increase in housing disputes would have been about 95. This is true also of general disputes between Koreans and Japanese, which increased from 116 in 1925 to 6,525 in 1933. SP155, pp. 174, 181; SUJ, 1933, pp. 1616, 1638. The Japanese government considered the Sōaikai and other peace and friendship groups to be failures: "These groups are little more than mere names and have little influence or strength." SUJ, 1933, p. 1399.

[87] See chapter vii, Note 18.

[88] SUJ, 1933, p. 1401.

IV

THE COMMUNIST AND NATIONALIST MOVEMENTS: THE FIRST PHASE

Japanese society was seething with discontent during the decade of the 1920's. A new and often radical labor movement was challenging management with an unprecedented number of strikes. The Suiheisha was rapidly uniting the members of the outcast class to protest their inferior positions in society. University students and professors opposed the government's new plan of military training in the schools. Developments such as these, as well as the activities of the communists and the anarchists, created a red scare that, at times, bordered on panic and led to severe governmental suppression of left-wing activity.

Koreans were held in contempt by the average Japanese, and this led to the suspicion that they were subversive. As early as the 1920's, even the Japanese government had come to regard all Koreans in Japan as potentially subversive. Japanese police kept a close watch on Korean leaders and organizations despite the fact that the majority of Koreans in Japan had no interest in plots, anti-Japanese or otherwise.

The Koreans as a Security Problem

Japanese police attended public meetings of Koreans and recorded their movements. In 1925, the Japanese police listed the names of 218 Koreans who were considered dangerous. Most of the blacklisted leaders lived in Tokyo (94), Osaka (67), and Kyoto (10) and the others in Hyogo, Aichi, and Hokkaido. Most of them were intellectuals; laborers numbered only twenty.[1] According to the Japanese police, 144 were nationalists, 70 communists, and 15 anarchists,[2] but this divsion is misleading since even those classified as communists and anarchists were Korean nationalists working for the freedom of their homeland.

Early Korean organizations in Japan had been mainly student associations formed for social and political purposes.[3] During the last years of the First World War, Korean laborers in Japan began to form their own societies. About a dozen Korean groups were active in Tokyo before 1919. By 1920, Korean associations were established in Osaka, Kyoto, and Kobe.[4] The number of Korean groups increased rapidly until by October, 1925, there were 161 different organizations.[5]

The associations of 1925 fall into five types: friendship and mutual aid, 75 groups; laborers' cooperatives, 30 groups; protection for laborers and self-supporting students, 14 groups; Japan-Korean friendship, 12 groups; free-the-

[1] SP155, pp. 48–49.
[2] *Ibid.*, p. 52.
[3] *Ibid.*, p. 65.
[4] *Ibid.*, p. 66.
[5] *Ibid.*, p. 65.

proletariat and "thought" research, 11 groups.[6] It was the last type that caused the Japanese authorities the most concern.

A great change in the complexion of Korean associations had taken place since 1922, a year when many labor and thought groups were organized.[7] The Japanese government maintained that the three main reasons for the rapid development of such groups were the increased numbers of Koreans who came to Japan after 1921, the Koreans' attempt to raise their educational level, and divisive factionalism within the associations.[8]

During the 1920's, the Korean leaders attempted to rally all Koreans in Japan around the banner of Korean nationalism in order to launch a unified movement. The nationalists joined Korean labor and thought groups and captured the leadership of any organization that would cooperate with them. Groups under their control usually had contact with left-wing Japanese organizations and with Koreans outside of Japan. Worried about Red plots to overthrow the government, the Japanese police were concerned about the increasing number of Korean communists and the threat of liaison between Japanese and Korean communists.[9]

The Korean Nationalist Movement

Although there was intensified activity among Korean nationalist leaders in Japan and Korean associations proliferated there, the Korean nationalist movement declined

---

[6] *Ibid.*, pp. 68–69. The five kinds of associations total 149. The documents give no explanation of the missing 19.
[7] *Ibid.*, p. 67.
[8] *Ibid.*, p. 68.
[9] *Ibid.*, pp. 55–56.

between 1921 and 1930.[10] The power of the provisional government in Shanghai waned rapidly and the various overseas nationalists groups argued bitterly.

At the time of the Washington Naval Conference in November, 1921, Korean students in Tokyo repeated their activities of February, 1919. They drafted a petition for independence and submitted it to both houses of the Japanese Diet, foreign embassies in Japan, and Koreans living abroad. About 300 students attended a rally, shouting, "Manse!" for Korean independence. They refused to attend school for a week as a protest against Japanese control of Korea.[11]

No foreign help was offered, however, and the Koreans in Japan and elsewhere began to realize that Korean independence was not going to be given to them as a gift by outsiders. Nationalist leaders decided that the only way to gain any form of independence was to strengthen Korea by enlightening the general population and by improving economic conditions. They called this new method "feeding their power."[12] This policy did not condone rash acts of violence, and although some Koreans in Japan and Shanghai continued to plan the assassination of Japanese leaders, most Korean leaders in Japan did not participate in the plans.

Each year on the first day of March, nationalist groups commemorated the events of the spring of 1919. The ceremony held in Tokyo in 1925 may be considered typical. The Ichigatsukai, the Chōsen Rōdō Sōdōmei (Korean Federation of Labor) and several other groups jointly sponsored the day's events. They had printed copies of a special song and

[10] Chong-sik Lee, "The Korean Nationalist Movement, 1905–1945" (unpublished doctoral dissertation), p. 464.
[11] SP155, pp. 187–188.
[12] Ibid., p. 187.

of political pamphlets but, ten minutes before the ceremony, Japanese police arrived and confiscated the printed material as well as four old Korean flags made of cloth and a dozen smaller ones made of paper. The first Korean speaker, a student from Waseda University, opened, "We honor this day on which six years ago our national existence was proclaimed. . . ."[13] The police regarded this statement as a violation of the Peace Preservation Law and ordered the meeting dissolved. The 250 Koreans present were forced to leave. Later on the same day they attempted to meet again in a different place, and 124 of them were arrested.[14]

Another annual meeting of Koreans in Japan was the memorial service for Koreans killed in the massacre following the Great Earthquake of September, 1923. Each year, Korean nationalist groups used this service to advance their cause. They spoke of the "slaughter" of Koreans by the Japanese, but urged Japanese sympathizers to attend the meetings.[15] The second annual memorial service was held in Tokyo on September 24, 1925, by the Ichigatsukai, the Chōsen Rōdō Sōdōmei, and seven other Korean groups. A few Japanese and about 800 Koreans attended the meeting. Police ordered them to take down the flags with "improper" characters written on them and repeatedly warned them to stop speaking on "improper" topics. Of the twenty-five people who made speeches, police silenced fifteen. Finally, they ordered the meeting closed.[16]

In Yokohama the police interrupted the memorial service when speakers began to give "exaggerated" accounts of the number of Koreans killed after the earthquake.[17] These were typical of Korean meetings held in Japan during

[13] *Ibid.*, p. 190.
[14] *Ibid.*, p. 191.
[15] *Ibid.*, p. 148.
[16] *Ibid.*, pp. 150–151.
[17] *Ibid.*, p. 153.

the 1920's. Koreans had to register the meeting in advance with the local police station, and the police were always in attendance; speakers were often silenced and frequently sent to jail.

Development of the Korean Communist Party in Japan

Some Koreans studying in Japan were strongly influenced by Japanese leftists, especially Marxists, and during the early 1920's, "more Korean Marxists were being made in Japan than were being made in Russia."[18] There were four main left-wing Korean thought groups in Tokyo in the early 1920's among the large number of Korean associations that had started by that time. In addition, left-wing labor groups had organized two associations, one in Tokyo and one in Osaka. Three of the thought groups were classified by the Japanese government as communist and one labor union in Tokyo was considered to be radical. These early groups might better be called "proto-communist," since they were a mixture of many elements. Led by students and intellectuals, the groups were often torn by factional disputes.[19]

In 1922, Korean students in Tokyo had organized the Hokuseikai (North Star Society) for the study of socialism. This group soon merged with another in Korea and used a new name, Kitakazekai (North Wind Society).[20] The newly combined group, using Japan as a base of operations, began to spread propaganda in Korea, and soon initiated

[18] Scalapino and Lee, "The Origins of the Korean Communist Movement (II)," 160.
[19] The various elements were held together by a common desire to obtain independence for Korea.
[20] Scalapino and Lee, "The Origins of the Korean Communist Movement (II)," 160.

a farmer-labor movement in the peninsula.[21] The cooperation between the Korean members in Japan and those in Korea lasted less than two years. In January, 1925, the group split and the Ichigatsukai was organized with members in Japan only.[22]

The Ichigatsukai wanted to create a new society with equality of classes and sexes, to make an organized effort to win the nationalist fight, and to supply the "people's government" with the proper ideology.[23] Together with the Tōkyō Chōsen Musan Seinen Dōmeikai (Tokyo Korean Proletarian Youth League), it was one of the two proto-Communist thought groups in Tokyo in 1925. Ichigatsukai cooperated with the communist group of Takatsu Masamichi and with the left-wing movement in Korea. In June, 1925, Takatsu's group and the Ichigatsukai jointly sponsored a lecture on social studies during which Takatsu's organization advocated freedom for Korea. The two groups worked closely together thereafter.[24]

[21] SP155, p. 77. This occurred in the summer of 1923.
[22] *Ibid.*, pp. 78, 89.
[23] *Ibid.*, p. 78.
[24] *Ibid.* Takatsu Masamichi had been engaged in left-wing activities from the time he was a student at Waseda University. He was one of the leaders of the Minjin Dōmeikai (People's Alliance), an association organized by faculty and students in 1919 to teach "democracy." Takatsu, because of his close association with the Nihon Shakaishugi Dōmei (Japanese Socialism League), was asked by the university authorities to leave school. As a result, the Minjin Dōmeikai came to an end in 1920. Takatsu's left-wing activities, however, were just beginning. He helped found two new groups, of which one, the Kōgai Sōshiki Gyōminkai, generally referred to as the Gyōminkai (Dawn People's Club), was to form the nucleus of Kondō Eizo's "communist party." Kondō, after conferring with Comintern agents in Shanghai in May, 1921, enlisted the aid of the Gyōminkai to form Japan's first Communist Party. The new but short-lived party, Gyōmin Kyōsantō (Dawn People's Communist Party), was composed of "enthusiastic students," and was never officially recognized by the Comintern. The new group printed and distributed subversive literature. In Novem-

The proto-communist thought group in Osaka, the Sanichi Musan Seinenkai (March First Proletarian Youth Society) organized in 1925, maintained close contact with both Japanese communists and socialists.[25] Its aims and those of the Tokyo Korean Proletarian Youth League were similar to those of the Ichigatsukai.[26]

The largest and most active left-wing Korean labor union was the Zainihon Chōsen Rōdō Sōdōmei (Federation of Labor of the Koreans in Japan). Established in February, 1925, this group attempted to organize all Korean laborers in Japan. It advocated a coalition with Nippon Rōdō Sōdōmei (Japan Federation of Labor).[27] The Zainihon Chōsen Rōdō Sōdōmei, or Rōsō, was destined to play a key role in the Korean communist movement. By 1929, the Japanese government considered this union the "most powerful fighting group among the Korean organizations in Japan."[28]

The number of Koreans belonging to these groups in 1925 was small. The total membership of the two proto-communist thought groups in Tokyo was only 92. The Sanichi Musan Seinenkai of Osaka had only ten members. Rōsō had a total membership of 1,580.[29] The Korean com-

---

ber the association dared to distribute antimilitaristic leaflets to troops taking part in maneuvers in the Tokyo area. The police acted quickly, and by December the first forty people were arrested. Thus ended the "prehistory" of the Japanese Communist Party. Swearingen and Langer, *Red Flag in Japan*, pp. 9–13. *Nihon kindaishi jiten*, pp. 125, 475–476, 584.

[25] The words "March First" referred to the March First Movement in Korea in 1919. SP155, pp. 95–96.

[26] The Tokyo Korean Proletarian Youth League advocated the destruction of the social system and the building of a new society. SP155, pp. 82–83.

[27] *Ibid.*, p. 108.

[28] SUJ, 1929, p. 27. Kim Ch'ŏn-hae (Kin Ten Kai), a leading postwar communist, headed this organization from about 1926 to 1929, when he was jailed by the Japanese police.

[29] SP155, pp. 71–72.

munist movement in Japan was far from being a mass movement of the 129,870 Koreans who were in Japan in the mid-1920's. These relatively small groups were still active enough to cause the Japanese police and government much concern.

Rōsō, a legally registered union, represented only part of the Korean communist organization in Japan. The underground or illegal part of the organization consisted of two groups, Chōsen Kyōsantō Nihon Sōkyoku (Korean Communist Party, Japan General Bureau) and Kōrai Kyōsan Seinenkai Nihonbu (Korean Communist Youth Society, Japan Section). A second legal group, the Zainihon Chōsen Seinen Dōmei (Korean Youth League in Japan), was organized on March 21, 1928.[30] Before 1929, these four groups were independent and had no systematic contacts with the Japanese Communist Party. The Korean communists, like the Japanese, were hard hit by the mass arrests in 1928 and 1929. Those connected in any way with the two underground sections of the Korean Communist Party were arrested or forced to flee. Many members of the two legal groups were also caught in the net cast by the Special Higher Police (Tokkō Keisatsu). Both of the illegal organizations were destroyed and the legal groups were temporarily disrupted.[31]

Government Reaction to Korean Radicalism

Alarmed at the rapid growth of Korean labor and thought groups after 1922, the Japanese government noted that they had not experienced such groups in Japan before.[32] The authorities responsible for internal security considered

[30] SUJ, 1933, p. 1455.
[31] *Ibid.*
[32] SP155, p. 67.

the dangerous possibility of a united front among dissident elements, and, indeed, their fears were realized later in the merger of the Korean and Japanese communist parties after 1929.

During the 1920's and into the 1930's, Japan experienced a prolonged, hysterical red scare and the government became obsessed by the need to destroy the "dangerous thought" being spread by left-wing movements. On May 12, 1925, just one week after manhood suffrage had been enacted in Japan, the Peace Preservation Law was promulgated. It was a drastic measure that gave the government a powerful weapon to combat its political foes. The new law provided that "anyone who has organized a society with the object of altering the national constitution (kokutai) or of repudiating the private property system, or anyone who has joined such an organization with full knowledge of its object shall be liable to imprisonment with or without hard labor for a term not exceeding ten years." [33]

The government, however, realized that for many Koreans, the "left-wing movement" and "nationalism" were different names for the same thing.[34] A report compiled by the police division of the Home Ministry cast some light on the matter of security. The report noted that "when students first come to Japan they are not mixed up with politics, but as time goes by their thought changes and they become bad students."[35] These "bad students" then attempted, according to the government, to infect the "simple fellows" who filled the ranks of the Korean laborers,

---

[33] *The Japan Yearbook, 1928*, pp. 277–278. The law contained seven articles. For a translation of the first three articles see Harold S. Quigley, *Japanese Government and Politics*, pp. 57–58. The Tokkō Keisatsu (Special Higher Police) was organized to enforce the law.
[34] SP155, p. 59.
[35] *Ibid.*, pp. 35–36.

and thus to gain control of the Korean labor movement in Japan.[36]

To prevent rebels from Shanghai smuggling themselves into Japan or Korea, the Japanese government maintained a network of spies in Shanghai. A close watch was kept on all ports in the Empire. Even so, Korean exiles occasionally managed to infiltrate Japan and lend their support and leadership to the Korean nationalist and left-wing organizations.

[36] During the late 1920's and early 1930's more of the leadership came from the ranks of Korean labor. This was especially true of the Korean communist movement.

V
THE COMMUNIST AND NATIONALIST MOVEMENT: THE SECOND PHASE

A discerning student of Japanese politics remarked in 1929 that "probably no country, not even America, is more obsessed with Bolshephobia than Japan."[1] The government responded to the threat of "dangerous thought" with increasingly repressive police controls.

The new government of Premier Tanaka Giichi began a systematic suppression of the communist movement in Japan when, on March 15, 1928, the police arrested more than 1,500 persons in a massive national roundup of left-wing elements. To aid the police in crushing the communist movement, the Peace Preservation Law was amended on June 29, 1928, to include the death penalty. On April 16, 1929, the police launched a second nationwide effort

[1] Kenneth Colegrove, "Labor Parties in Japan," *The American Political Science Review*, XXIII (May, 1929), 359.

to eradicate the left wing and arrested more than a thousand persons.[2]

As a result of the anti-communist campaign, the Nihon Kyōsantō (Japanese Communist Party) was forced completely underground. The party next turned its attention to the working masses and illegally organized the Nippon Rōdō Kumiai Zenkoku Kyōgikai, or Zenkyō (National Conference of Japanese Trade Unions), on December 25, 1928.[3] It was at this critical time that the Korean Communist Party in Japan decided to unite with the Japanese Communist Party.[4]

Before 1929 the Korean Communist Party in Japan was controlled by extreme left-wing elements in Korea. Korean communists sometimes cooperated with individual Japanese communists, but there was no systematic liason with the Japanese movement.[5] By 1929, both Korean and Japanese communists were in the mood for amalgamation. The Japanese communists were trying to create a mass base for support, and in the face of the government's determination to destroy the party, it was clear that the Japanese communists should consider closer cooperation with their Korean counterparts. Both parties had suffered extensive damage during the mass arrests of left-wingers during 1928 and 1929.[6]

The first official platform of the Japanese Communist Party advocated "complete independence for the (Japanese) colonies,"[7] a program which would attract Korean

[2] Rodger Swearingen and Paul Langer, *Red Flag in Japan*, pp. 27–37.
[3] *Ibid.*, p. 36.
[4] SUJ, 1933, p. 1455.
[5] *Ibid.*
[6] *Ibid.*
[7] Swearingen and Langer, *Red Flag in Japan*, p. 25. After Kazama Jōkichi returned from Moscow to assume leadership of the Japanese

communists who were ardent nationalists first and communists second.[8] During 1929 and 1930, the formerly independent Korean communist movement merged with the Japanese party. At first, the Koreans occupied minor positions in the party hierarchy, but by 1932, they had advanced to the inner circles.[9] By 1933, more than half of the members of Zenkyō were Koreans, who had so firm a grip on the union and the party leadership that the Japanese communists found it impossible to act without their cooperation.[10] The Korean communists in Japan used Zenkyō and the party as an operational base from which to rebuild the shattered Communist Party in their homeland.[11]

communists, in late 1930, he emphasized bringing the Koreans and the Taiwanese into the communist movement. In April, 1931, after his return to Japan, he produced "The Japanese Communist Party Political Thesis — a Draft," calling for the "complete independence of colonial places such as Korea and Taiwan." In May the central committee proclaimed a "nationalities policy" ("racial policy," minzoku seisaku), implemented by a new nationalities section which was to "contact and support the Communist movements in Korea and Taiwan, and to organize the Koreans and Taiwanese who lived in Japan." In his effort to enlist the aid of Japan's colonial subjects, Kazama was quite successful. In July, 1932, Kim Ch'i-jŏng (see note 20 below) and a Taiwanese became reporters in the nationalities section, and thousands of Koreans joined either the party or Zenkyō. The Japanese Communist Party worked hard to secure new members from among the Koreans living in Japan. Their newspaper *Akahata* (Red Flag) and other publications spread propaganda among the Koreans. On August 30, 1932, *Akahata* urged the Kansai area committee to redouble its efforts to enlist Koreans, Taiwanese, and Chinese laborers. Shihōshō keijikyoku, *Chōsenjin no kyōsanshugi undō*, p. 143.

[8] Robert A. Scalapino and Chong-sik Lee, "The Origins of the Korean Communist Movement (II)," *The Journal of Asian Studies*, XX (February, 1961), 164. SP155, p. 53.

[9] SUJ, 1933, p. 1457.

[10] *Ibid.*, p. 1540.

[11] *Ibid.*, p. 1586.

The Unified Communist Movement

In 1929, the unified movement of the Japanese and Korean communist parties began. Rōsō, the communist Federation of Labor of the Koreans in Japan, soon recovered from the police raids of 1928 and 1929. In 1929 its membership jumped to 23,530, with nine affiliated unions under its banner. The union was more active than ever in spreading communist propaganda and recruiting new members.[12]

At a nationwide rally held on December 14, 1929, in Osaka, the leadership of Rōsō decided to abandon the organization's independent status. The delegates agreed that it was a mistake to remain under the leadership of the Communist Party in Korea. They would unite with the Japanese communists in an effort to gain power in Japan. The delegates made it clear that they were working primarily for the independence of Korea and not for the progress of international communism. "For the pure racial freedom of Korea our premise must be to have the support of the Japanese Communist Party. . . . Therefore, we need to join Zenkyō, which is under the Japanese Communist Party, and make a common fight."[13] The unification of Japanese and Korean left-wing groups, which the Japanese police had feared for a decade, was finally accomplished.

Most of the branch unions of the old Rōsō dissolved in 1930; by the end of October of that year, more than 2,600 from the old Rōsō had joined Zenkyō and 7,600 had joined affiliated organizations. The old Rōsō organization retained a membership of 5,000.[14] Despite the mass arrests, Zenkyō continued to grow and so did the percentage of Koreans that were members. By the end of October, 1931, the total mem-

[12] SUJ, 1929, p. 27.
[13] *Ibid.*, 1930, p. 21.
[14] The figures do not total 23,550, for many members had been arrested. SUJ, 1930, p. 22.

bership was 10,700 and, of this number, more than 4,100 were Koreans.[15] The activities of Zenkyō and the number of police arrests both reached a peak in 1933, with 1,820 apprehensions.

Most students and intellectuals who joined Zenkyō had worked in left-wing movements in Korea. By 1932 they had infiltrated the center of the union. The greatest number of new members were Koreans who were the most active in "front-line" work such as handing out pamphlets.[16] In Tokyo it was mainly the Korean leaders who were working to rebuild Zenkyō, as the police strove to destroy it. In Osaka the Koreans were in virtual control of the organization.[17]

Attempt to Rebuild the Communist Party in Korea

The first official Korean Communist Party had been formed in Seoul on April 17, 1925. The young party had been in operation for a little more than six months when the Japa-

[15] *Ibid.*, 1931, p. 4.
[16] *Ibid.*, 1933, p. 1457.
[17] *Ibid.*, pp. 1539–1540. In 1929 and 1930 most Korean members of Zenkyō held subordinate positions in the union. As the older Japanese members were arrested, however, Koreans began to assume more important positions. By 1932 they were controlling the area and branch associations, and held top positions in the public works section. During the mass arrests of 1933 the Korean grip on the union became even tighter. Nine Koreans were chairmen of the standing committees for public works, publications, chemicals, and metals. Many Korean union officials also were members of the Japanese Communist Party or the Communist Youth Association. Zenkyō was the heart of the left-wing organizations in the Kansai, and the Koreans dominated its Osaka and Tokyo headquarters. *Chōsenjin no kyōsanshugi undō*, pp. 107–142. This document gives a detailed account of the role played by the Koreans. Korean members of the Japanese Communist Party played a similar role, taking over higher positions as the Japanese leaders were arrested. *Ibid.*, pp. 143–151.

nese police on the peninsula imprisoned most of its members.[18] Every attempt to revive the party had been thwarted by the police.

Kim Ch'i-jŏng, a Korean member of the Japanese Communist Party, made a strong effort to reestablish the party in Korea, using Japan as a base. While in Shanghai in 1929, Kim had joined a union under Zenkyō and began to make plans to rebuild the Korean Communist Party in the peninsula. On his return to Japan, he sought the aid of the Japanese Communist Party. In July, 1932, in his official capacity as reporter in the party's new nationalities section, he requested support for his project.

Konno Yojirō and other members of the party's central committee approved Kim's plan. Konno said, "If there are superior people among the Koreans the Japanese Communist Party must help them. Many Japanese have moved to Korea and most Korean enterprises are owned by them. . . . The fighting in Korea must be a cooperative fight with the Koreans and Japanese helping each other. The Japanese people in Korea are easy to organize. We will send back to Korea a really expert Korean comrade to organize them."[19] The "expert Korean comrade" Konno had in mind was Kim.

While cultivating contacts within the Japanese Communist Party, Kim was also actively engaged in gaining support from left-wing Korean groups. At first, he attempted to work through the Korean anarchists, but eventually he created his own front group, the Rōdō Kaikyūsha (Labor

[18] Scalapino and Lee, "The Origins of the Korean Communist Movement (II)," pp. 161–163.
[19] SUJ, 1933, p. 1586. Konno had returned from Moscow in the early fall of 1930. Only a month after he had made this statement supporting Kim's project, Konno was arrested by the Japanese police. Swearingen and Langer, *Red Flag in Japan*, pp. 44, 55. The phrase, "expert Korean comrade," can also be translated in the plural.

Class Association), which functioned as a cover for his secret Chōsen Kyōsantō Saiken Tōsō Kyōgikai (Council to Fight for the Renewal of the Korean Communist Party). The latter group held secret meetings and published a newspaper, Rōdō Kaikyū (Labor Class). Kim sent many organizers to Korea who were to gain control of the scattered left-wing movement and prepare the ground for his return in September, 1932. When Kim had nearly completed his preparations in Japan in August, he dispatched ten more agents to Korea. Soon after the agents left, the Japanese police struck. Kim and fourteen others were arrested in Tokyo. In January, 1933, the drama came to an end when the police arrested the last three members of Kim's group. All the men arrested were also members of the Japanese Communist Party.[20]

Just before its collapse in the mid-1930's, the Japanese Communist Party experienced a brilliant Indian summer of revitalization. From the summer of 1931 to the fall of 1932, membership increased to an all-time high as the party quick-

[20] SUJ, 1933, pp. 1457, 1585–1586. Kim Ch'i-jŏng and several other Koreans fled Japan in March, 1928, to escape a mass arrest of communists. In Shanghai, Kim's group cooperated with other left-wing Koreans in publishing a magazine. By March, 1929, they had created the Kōrai Kyōsan Seinen Dōmei (Korean Communist Youth League). Kim and his followers planned to return to Japan and to rebuild the Korean Communist Party in their homeland. SUJ, 1932, p. 1504; ibid., 1933, p. 1586. One of the Korean participants in this project has written an incomplete but interesting account of the episode. See Sam-kyu Kim, Chōsen no shinjitsu, pp. 11–12. The seven membership rules for the two organizations led by Kim reflect the spirit of their leader and the dedication of these Koreans to their cause: "(1) You must give your publications, finances, and prestige to the organization; (2) you must keep our secrets even under pain of death; (3) you must pay monthly dues of fifty sen; (4) you must obey the rules of the democratically centralized administrative system; (5) we must have a unified organization, and decisions are to be made by voting; (6) if you are more than three minutes late for a regular meeting you will be expelled; and (7) you must have no close ties with your family." SUJ, 1933, pp. 1587–1588.

ened its propaganda offensive. Mass arrests came, however, in the fall of 1932, and from then until 1935, the party organization gradually fell apart.[21] As the Japanese leaders were apprehended and sent to prison, Korean party members replaced them. The Koreans came close to seizing control of the entire organization,[22] but they too were paying a heavy toll to police raids. In 1933, the peak year for arrests of Korean communists in Japan, 1,820 were apprehended. The next year the number was 834. By 1935 it had dropped to 232, and in 1936, only 193 Korean communists were arrested.[23] When the party finally disintegrated, the Korean members were jailed or put under strict surveillance. Some feeble attempts were made by former party members to rebuild Zenkyō, but they failed and the Korean communist movement in Japan remained dormant until after the end of the Second World War.[24]

The Nationalist Movement

In Korea and Japan, the years between 1927 and 1931 were a period of close cooperation between the nationalists and the communists, a coalition which reached a point of phenomenal strength in the peninsula.[25] After 1931, however, the communist and noncommunist camps grew increasingly hostile toward each other, and active cooperation ceased. The Manchurian Incident of September, 1931, stimulated Korean nationalists[26] and the provisional government in Shanghai to renewed activity.

[21] Swearingen and Langer, *Red Flag in Japan*, pp. 57–58.
[22] SUJ, 1933, p. 1414.
[23] *Ibid.*, 1936, p. 1449.
[24] *Ibid.*, p. 1450. Swearingen and Langer, *Red Flag in Japan*, pp. 67–68.
[25] *Ibid.*, pp. 249–250.
[26] SUJ, 1932, pp. 5–6; Lee, *The Politics of Korean Nationalism*, pp. 179, 200, 201.

Korean rebels in Shanghai started the year 1932 with renewed efforts to assassinate high Japanese officials. A Korean resident in Japan, under the direction of Kim Ku, then head of the Korean Provisional Government, made an attempt on the life of the Emperor in Tokyo. The January 8 attempt is called the Sakuradamon Incident after the place where it occurred. The would-be assassin, a laborer named Yi Pong-ch'ang (alias Asayama Shōichi), was provided with money and two hand grenades by the provisional government in Shanghai. After his return to Japan, Yi spent several weeks moving around Tokyo trying to discover a way to carry out the assassination. The official report of the police, who traced every move he made, reveals that Yi was unsuccessful in formulating a real plan. One day while riding a streetcar he learned, by chance, that the Emperor would leave the palace for a few hours on January 8 to review troops at the Yoyogi parade ground. After several misadventures, Yi was nearly arrested by the police but was saved by a card of introduction bearing the name of a sergeant in the military police. Yi finally found himself in the midst of a large crowd waiting for the Imperial procession. Behind him towered the building that housed the Metropolitan Police Board. As the carriages began to pass by, Yi realized that he had no idea which one contained the Emperor. He threw a grenade at the wrong carriage. He had missed the Emperor by a hundred feet. A few seconds later he was seized by the chief of police and thrown into jail.[27]

Yi's attempt only enraged the Japanese populace. The authorities responsible for security also hardened their attitude toward Koreans. The incident occurred just when the Korean communists were becoming very active in the Japanese communist movement. The Inukai Tsuyoshi cabinet

[27] SUJ, 1932, pp. 1514–1516; *Trans-Pacific*, January 14, 1932, p. 10.

was nearly forced to resign and "a storm of protest" arose when it failed to do so.[28]

As the Korean nationalist fervor increased, however, so did the activities of the Japanese police. A division of the police bureau of the Home Ministry concerned itself exclusively with the Korean social movement. The reports compiled by the ministry at times gave the impression that the police bureau had a better overall view of the Korean national movement than the Koreans themselves had.

Statistics published by the police bureau partially reveal the strength of the nationalist movement. The number of Koreans apprehended for violation of the Peace Preservation Law was as follows:[29]

1933	1,820	1937	144	1942	168
1934	834	1938	117	1943	144
1935	232	1939	50	1944	189
1936	193	1940	165	1945	81
		1941	257		

The total for 1933 is highest because of the flurry of activity by Korean members of the Japanese Communist Party.

The Korean nationalists were not very active in 1933, but those in Japan continued to keep in contact with the rebels in Shanghai and to distribute seditious printed matter.[30] The number of Korean groups and their membership illus-

[28] *Trans-Pacific*, January 14, 1932, p. 15. The cabinet was expected to accept the responsibility for anything that occurred in the Empire. The cabinet of Admiral Yamamoto Gonbei (September 2, 1923–January 7, 1924) had resigned after an attempt was made on the life of the Prince Regent.
[29] The tabulation was compiled from three sources: SUJ, 1936, p. 1449; *ibid.*, 1942, p. 834; and Naimushō keihokyoku, *Nendobetsu Chōsenjin chiihō ihan kenkyo shirabe sono ta*, p. 93359.
[30] SUJ, 1933, p. 1601.

trate the decline of the communist element in the Korean nationalist movement after 1933.[31]

	1933 Groups	1933 Members	1936 Groups	1936 Members
Communist	113	10,943	46	901
Nationalist	182	22,564	301	19,508

The army coup of February 26, 1936, in Tokyo, combined with the victory of a Korean in the marathon at the Berlin Olympic Games in 1936, infused the nationalist movement with new vigor. The Chōsenjin Mondai Kyōgikai (Korean Problems Conference Association) was organized in Kyoto; in Hyogo, the movement to unify the Korean groups in Japan began to make progress.[32]

In the eyes of the Japanese police, the most dangerous nationalist movement was a new group, the Aikoku Seinen Kai (Patriotic Youth Association), established in February, 1936, as a secret organization with only five members, who were convinced that war was the prelude to independence, that Koreans must prepare for the revolution now, and that they must themselves provide the leadership.[33] The five also led a labor-union organization, the Izumi Ippan Rōdō Kumiai (Izumi General Labor Association), organized on October 1, 1930. It was known to the Japanese police as the main nationalistic organization in Osaka. This "union" had originally been connected with Zenkyō, but because of

[31] The tabulation is based upon two sources: SUJ, 1933, p. 1413; ibid., 1936, p. 1401.
[32] The Korean nationalists thought they might gain advantage from the confusion they hoped would result from the attempted coup. For Korean feeling in regard to the Olympic victory see Lee, *The Politics of Korean Nationalism*, pp. 262–263. SUJ, 1936, p. 1480.
[33] Ibid., pp. 1481–1482.
[34] Ibid., p. 1480.

police pressure, had cut its ties to avoid the fate which befell Zenkyō.[34] Two of the five Koreans established an illegal school in one of the union's branch offices in Sakai in February, 1932. The school, which had as many as forty laborers enrolled at one time, taught the history of Korea and of the Indian independence movement. Within a month the Special Higher Police had moved in and destroyed the entire organization.[35]

After the North China incident of 1937 and the expansion of the war on the mainland of Asia, the Japanese police kept a close watch on Korean students and intellectuals in Japan. The police complained that the Korean students lacked interest in the North China incident and felt that they did not want Japan to win the war.[36]

Most educated Koreans continued to be cool toward Japan's war aims and many of them harassed the Japanese and the Koreans who were aiding the Japanese war efforts. They wrote articles condemning the Japanese for discrimination and misrule in Korea and inscribed anti-Japanese and pro-Korean slogans on the walls of buildings. They started thousands of "dangerous" rumors designed to hurt Japan's war effort by undermining the confidence of the people.[37] They said, for example, that the press was not printing the truth about troop losses and that the Chinese were stronger than the Japanese. During 1939, the police investigated thirty-four major and many minor incidents of seditious rumors spread by Koreans.[38]

After the beginning of the Greater East Asian War in

[35] *Ibid.*, p. 1481.
[36] *Ibid.*, 1937, p. 6; "Korean Red Group of University Students Arrested in Tokyo Independence Movement," *The Japan Chronicle*, October, 1938, p. 415.
[37] Chong-sik Lee, *The Politics of Korean Nationalism*, pp. 246–247.
[38] SUJ, 1939, p. 966. See also Naimushō keihokyoku hoanka, *Hokushi jihen ni kansuru jōhō*, pp. 172–178, 193–194.

1941, some Korean students and intellectuals continued to criticize the Japanese war effort and to commit seditious acts. Korean nationalists saw Japan's further involvement in the war as an opportunity for eventual freedom.[39] The number of Koreans arrested for violations of the Peace Preservation Law was five times as great in 1941 as in 1939.[40] The 165 persons arrested in 1940 included 86 middle-school students.[41] The government was convinced, in 1942, that the students and intellectuals were secretly hoping that Japan would lose the war,[42] for they continued to spread wild rumors and to write seditious slogans on public walls.[43]

Many Koreans in Japan, however, were not actively anti-Japanese. Numerous laborers cooperated with the Japanese by raising money and giving free labor for the war effort; some even volunteered for military service.[44] Whether by gentle persuasion, for example, by the Kyōwakai, or Concordia Association, or real desire, Koreans in Japan contributed to the war effort. By August, 1937, Koreans had collected more than 10,000 yen to give to the government, and Korean groups and individuals were requesting that they be allowed to serve in the armed forces.[45] Some young Koreans were so anxious to serve the Emperor that they sent letters written in their own blood (kessho) to the government, requesting military duty.[46]

After the beginning of the Second World War, Koreans

[39] SUJ, 1941, p. 4; *Ibid.*, 1942, p. 4; SUJ, 1936, p. 1480; *Ibid.*, 1942, pp. 777–778; Lee, *The Politics of Korean Nationalism*, pp. 201, 277.
[40] See the tabulation on p. oo.   (ms. p. 61)
[41] SUJ, 1942, p. 778.
[42] *Ibid.*
[43] *Ibid.*, p. 841. This document describes 39 incidents in detail. *Ibid.*, pp. 841–855.
[44] SUJ, 1939, p. 966.
[45] At this time the Koreans in Japan could neither volunteer nor be drafted for military service. *Hokushi jihen ni kansuru jōhō*, p. 82.
[46] *Ibid.*

in Japan were even more cooperative. During 1942 they contributed 379,954 yen for national defense. Labor without compensation was given by 37,744 workers, and 658 groups (with 47,952 members) prayed to the gods that Japan would win the war.[47] When Tokyo was bombed on April 18, 1942, the ministry noted that most Koreans cooperated and some did an "outstanding job." The report suggested that the enemy attack had given them an incentive for supporting the war effort.[48]

Japanese Response to the Nationalist Movement

After years of neglect and half measures, the Japanese central government suddenly seemed to realize that the Kyōwakai, started as "friendship associations," would make an excellent tool for controlling the Koreans. In June, 1939, the police created the Chūō Kyōwakai (Central Concordia Association) to head the 37 friendship groups already established. Sekiya Teizaburō became chairman of the board of directors of the new organization,[49] which was controlled by the Japanese police. The police and the Kyōwakai worked closely together.[50] In some places policemen became the formal heads of the Kyōwakai,[51] and the headquarters of each of the 37 groups was located in a government building. The one in Osaka, for instance, was in the city government building, social section.[52]

In 1939 the Home Ministry felt that the new Kyōwakai was progressing well. This was the same ministry which in

[47] SUJ, 1942, pp. 839–840.
[48] Ibid., p. 855.
[49] Ibid., 1939, p. 1014.
[50] Ibid.
[51] Ibid.
[52] Ibid., pp. 1014–1017.

1933 had called the old Kyōwakai system a failure. The ministry added a pessimistic note in 1939, however, by declaring that the intellectuals and students still wanted racial freedom, and that the time "was still far away" when Japanese and Koreans would truly form one body.[53]

As the momentum of the war increased, the government tightened controls over the Koreans in Japan. The Kyōwakai operation was greatly expanded, and, by 1943, the 37 groups had been enlarged to 47, with still others in Karafuto. The 47 groups controlled 1,124 subgroups.[54] The central Kyōwakai asserted that the Koreans were becoming "patriotic Japanese citizens."[55]

In Seoul, the government-general organized the Chōsen Shōgakukai (Korean Study Aid Association), which in turn opened a branch office in Tokyo. This new organization cooperated with the Home Ministry and other branches of the Japanese government in supervising and helping Korean students, primarily to obtain employment.[56]

In 1943 the Japanese government made student travel to Japan much less attractive. New immigration regulations stipulated that Korean students entering the home islands must not harbor "dangerous," or anti-Japanese, thoughts. The students had to meet high academic standards and were required to have enough money to pay school expenses. They could be deported if they spoke against the war effort, engaged in "bad conduct," or absented themselves from school. All students had to belong to a student group of about 50, led by a professor or graduate student. The groups were to have close contact with the Kyōwakai, and the cen-

[53] *Ibid.*, p. 888.
[54] Naimushō keihokyoku hoanka, *Kyōwa jigyō kankei*, p. 90086.
[55] *Ibid.*
[56] SUJ, 1942, p. 741.

tral Kyōwakai was ordered to give them maximum supervision.[57]

As Japan moved from one military success to another, many Koreans began to feel that the wisest course would be cooperation. Koreans supported Japan's actions in Manchuria where the Japanese army acted as the protector of Korean migrant farmers in their disputes with Chinese.[58] Japanese expansion on the continent also allowed Koreans to move into governmental positions, especially in Manchuria. Japanese imperialism allowed talented Koreans to hold positions in the government, the army, and the police.

Whether the Koreans aided the Japanese war effort willingly or grudgingly is a question which cannot be answered with complete certainty. By the late 1930's, however, many Korean independence leaders had decided that further resistance was futile. Hence it was not surprising that many Koreans in Japan should cooperate with the Japanese. As Lee Chong-sik notes, "Because the pressure of the government upon Korean nationalist leaders was especially strong, many of them eventually yielded to it and became collaborators with the Japanese. As Tocqueville acutely observed a century ago, patriotism is not durable in a conquered nation." [59] A considerable number of nationalists did, however, manage to survive the war years, though some went to prison for their beliefs.

[57] Naimushō keihokyoku hoanka, *Kyōwakai kankei kaigi shorui shōgakukai kankei o fukumu*, p. 87173.
[58] Lee, *The Politics of Korean Nationalism*, pp. 182–183.
[59] Lee, *The Politics of Korean Nationalism*, p. 238.

VI

THE EFFECT OF JAPAN'S WAR EFFORTS ON THE KOREAN MIGRANTS

The lengthy war between China and Japan, which had been precipitated by the Manchurian Incident of 1931, brought about the rapid expansion of Japanese industry. To facilitate industry's increasing need for labor after 1937, the Japanese government began a systematic program that led in two years to a fuller mobilization of the nation's labor force.[1]

As the war in China increased in scope, the army began to drain the skilled Japanese workers from factories and mines. Korean labor was seen as a partial solution to the problem. The Japanese government first encouraged and then forced Koreans to come to Japan, thereby creating conflict with the government-general of Korea, which had con-

---

[1] Kazuo Okochi, *Labor in Modern Japan*, pp. 64–67.

sistently failed to fulfill its quota of laborers for the industrial machine across the straits.[2]

The Korean population in Japan increased sharply as a result of the war. In 1933 there were 456,217 Koreans in Japan,[3] and, by the end of 1936, there were 690,503.[4] At the end of the war the total was 2,400,000.[5]

From the late 1920's to 1939 there had been a gradual change in the composition of the Korean minority. Those who came to Japan during the early and middle 1920's were mostly young unmarried men who planned to stay just long enough to make some money to take home. After a season's work they would return to Korea for the New Year's festival or the Obon (Festival of the Dead) in midsummer. After 1931, when Japanese industry was gradually recovering from its depressed state, the Koreans found greater economic opportunity in Japan. The Japanese government encouraged the immigration of Korean married couples in the hope of creating a more stable Korean minority. In 1925, Korean males outnumbered females seven to one; by 1939, however, the figure was one and a half to one;[6] 88 per cent of the Koreans were living in family units.[7] The percentage of Koreans staying in one location for more than 90 days had greatly increased.[8] Koreans were beginning to be "permanent residents rather than temporary."[9] An American missionary who had been working with Koreans since 1906 commented, "Eight years ago one seldom

[2] Such conflicts were nothing new. For another example see Harold S. Quigley, *Japanese Government and Politics*, pp. 314–315.
[3] SUJ, 1933, p. 1397.
[4] *Ibid.*, 1936, p. 1371.
[5] *Nihon kindaishi jiten*, p. 217.
[6] SP155, p. 22. SUJ, 1939, p. 890.
[7] SUJ, 1939, p. 890.
[8] The tabulation is a composite of statistics from SUJ, 1933, p. 1399; 1936, pp. 1372–1373; and 1939, p. 890.
[9] *Ibid.*, 1939, p. 890.

	1933	*1936*	*1939*
Remained in one place more than 90 days	115,053	602,223	836,904
Remained in one place less than 90 days	47,477	88,278	124,687

met an old Korean over here. Now we see them everywhere — good evidence that the family has come to stay."[10]

After 1939 the trend toward permanence in housing and jobs was reversed by the influx of labor that came to man the Japanese war machine. By 1942 the number of people living in family groups had dropped to 75 per cent, the ratio of males to females had increased, and the number of people staying in one place more than 90 days had declined.[11]

	1931	*1939*	*1942*
Men	244	150	174
Women	100	100	100

Mobilization of the Korean Labor Force

Just before the Manchurian incident of 1931, Japan had approximately 3,000,000 unemployed. The Home Ministry was being pressured to cut off Korean immigration into Japan. The Manchurian Incident so stimulated the economy that within three to four years this situation was beginning to change. From 1933 to 1936 the yearly increase in the demand for labor was double the number of new workers available.[12] By May, 1937, there was a scarcity of

[10] R. L. Young, "Koreans in Japan," *The Korean Mission Field*, XXXII (April, 1936), 69.

[11] The figures are from SUJ, 1942, pp. 737–738.

[12] *The Oriental Economist*, August, 1938, pp. 18–19. See also the issue of May, 1936, p. 294. The drop in unemployment was a gradual process spread over several years. A Home Ministry report for 1933 mentioned that the influx of Korean labor was making the unemployment problem worse. SUJ, 1933, p. 1400.

labor.[13] As the demands on the economy increased, the government added to working hours, abolished age limits, and relaxed employment restrictions.[14]

As Japan's war on the continent expanded after 1937, the government drew up a comprehensive mobilization plan for the entire nation. In March, 1938, the Diet passed the National General Mobilization Act, which covered every foreseeable need and thus eliminated future specific legislation.[15] In effect, the Diet had signed and presented the government with a blank check. To implement the new law, the government in power had only to obtain an Imperial ordinance.

The Labor Mobilization Law, based on the mobilization act, which brought hundreds of thousands of Korean laborers to Japan between 1939 and 1945,[16] was promulgated by the government in August, 1939. During the first few years the government asked for volunteers, but later Koreans were conscripted.[17]

The government planned to bring in 907,697 Korean laborers from 1939 to 1945, but only 73 per cent of the quota

---

[13] *The Oriental Economist*, May, 1937, p. 263.
[14] *Ibid.*, August, 1941, p. 405.
[15] Hugh Borton, *Japan since 1931*, p. 62.
[16] SUJ, 1939, p. 5. In May, 1939, the *Asahi*, a large newspaper in Tokyo, reported that some members of the cabinet objected to the mass importation of Korean labor, and that the welfare minister and the home minister were "not in agreement" in regard to plans for importation of labor. The paper also noted that "under a labor policy of many years standing there have been police restrictions on mass importation of Korean labor." Article translated in *Trans-Pacific*, May 18, 1939, p. 9.
[17] Volunteers were taken whenever available, but the law did provide for conscription if not enough volunteers were obtained. Both volunteers and conscripts usually had a two-year tour of duty in Japan. SUJ, 1942, p. 761. It was not until 1942 that the Koreans in Japan became subject to conscription. Jerome B. Cohen, *Japan's Economy in War and Reconstruction*, p. 315.

Japan's War Effort and Korean Migrants

was filled.[18] About the time of the Manchurian crisis, the government-general of Korea had begun to promote industrial expansion in northern Korea. As a result of this new program, there was active competition, after 1934, with the home islands for the surplus labor available in southern Korea. In 1937 the government-general was luring workers to the north of Korea by granting reduced railway fares. Officials in Pusan interviewed laborers going to Japan and encouraged those without prior commitments to remain in Korea.[19]

The Welfare Ministry planned to transport 85,000 Korean laborers to Japan during 1939, but only 38,959 applied for jobs and only 19,135 actually went.[20] Most of them were sent to the mines of Hokkaido (7,053), Fukuoka (5,823), Fukushima (1,044), and Saga prefectures (1,203).[21] Some of the newly arrived laborers soon tired of the drab life and hard work of a coal miner; 400 deserted the mines and disappeared into Japan's cities.[22]

New laborers were generally given three months' training before being assigned to a job. The government encouraged employers to provide good living conditions, and ordinarily there was no difference in the pay of skilled Japanese and Korean workers.[23] Despite these precautions, the new laborers were continually embroiled in disputes with Japanese labor and management. Thirty-two disputes broke out in 1939 involving 4,140 Korean laborers. The Koreans were discontented because they had anticipated better working conditions, and felt that coal mining was too dangerous.

[18] *Ibid.*, p. 325.
[19] *Annual Report on Administration of Tyosen, 1937–38*, p. 109.
[20] These laborers came to Japan under the provisions of the Labor Mobilization Law of 1939. SUJ, 1939, p. 997.
[21] *Ibid.*, pp. 999–1000.
[22] *Ibid.*, p. 998.
[23] *Ibid.*, p. 1001.

There was also the inevitable friction between Japanese and Korean laborers because of differences in language and customs. The government suggested that the Koreans were growing presumptuous because they had been treated so well.[24]

By far the greatest number of disputes in 1939 occurred in Hokkaido [25] and were based on Korean complaints about their pay scale, living quarters, and food. One group threatened to leave their jobs if their demand for a 3 per cent pay raise was not met. Another group of 293 Korean miners declared that their food was fit only for pigs; at the climax of this dispute more than a hundred of the miners marched to the local police station and demanded return passage to Korea. A third strike was precipitated by a fight between Korean miners and their Japanese bosses; this dispute arose because many Koreans did not speak Japanese.[26]

In some parts of Japan the Japanese workers feared that they might be replaced by Korean contract labor. Japanese coal miners on Hokkaido sometimes objected to working with Koreans because the latter were unskilled in coal mining and lowered the wages of Japanese miners.[27] Others complained that they were being discriminated against and that Korean laborers were treated better.[28]

The Kyōwakai and Korean Labor

In 1936 there were 679 Korean peace and friendship groups with 78,846 members, but these groups were often inactive or, even worse from the government's point of view, served

[24] *Ibid.*, pp. 1001–1002.
[25] *Ibid.*, p. 1003.
[26] The total number of disputes for Hokkaido was 27. *Ibid.*, pp. 1003–1008.
[27] *Ibid.*, p. 1012.
[28] *Ibid.*, 1942, p. 910.

to cloak Korean nationalist movements.[29] The central government created the Kyōwa Jigyō (Concordia Enterprise) in 1936 and talked of using it to control the Koreans, but neglected to create a central organization to coordinate the 37 groups scattered throughout Japan (there were many subgroups). Fifteen months after the Diet passed the National General Mobilization Act, the government finally acted by creating the Chūō Kyōwakai (Central Concordia Association),[30] which was seen as the perfect instrument to control the large number of Koreans coming to Japan.

Even with the efforts of the Kyōwa Jigyō, the government's problems with Korean immigrant laborers increased rather than decreased between 1939 and 1942. The number of disputes rose to 787 and involved 49,532 people, roughly one-fifth of the total number of laborers who came to Japan under the provisions of the Labor Mobilization Law.[31] The government was frustrated also by its inability to obtain the 374,800 laborers it had requisitioned; only 248,521 came to Japan.[32] Of this number, 89,840 ran away and only 10,395 were caught by the police. As the war spread and the need for labor became more acute, the government had to face the fact that its immigrant labor plan was not working well.

To stop the Korean unrest and to prevent others from deserting their jobs, the government tightened its controls. New workers were given a more thorough preliminary training, and known agitators were apprehended and deported to Korea. Stronger controls were placed on daily workers and labor brokers as well as on Japanese companies employing Koreans. All Korean laborers were ordered to

[29] *Ibid.*, 1936, p. 1510.
[30] See "Japanese Response to the Nationalist Movement," in chap. iv.
[31] SUJ, 1942, p. 890.
[32] *Ibid.*, p. 889. The 1942 report uses the term "applying" (ōbo) for work as a laborer in Japan rather than "requisitioned" (chōyō).

wear a Kyōwakai membership badge, and this association was instructed to cooperate with the police in finding escapees.[33] From August 15 to October 15, 1942, the police checked 643,416 Korean laborers in all parts of Japan and found 68,468 without the required badge.[34]

By 1943 the revitalized Kyōwakai had increased to forty-seven groups with 1,124 branches.[35] Every Korean laborer automatically became a member of the organization when he came to Japan to work. The Kyōwakai's main concern was to make the Korean laborers "soldiers for industry." The association supervised their training period and followed up by sending teams of inspectors to factories and mines throughout Japan. After consulting with the management to check working conditions, the inspectors held "friendly discussions," encouraging the Koreans to remain at the same job, and talked individually with each man whose contract was due to expire.[36]

The association published a weekly newspaper, the *Kyōwa Shinbun* (45,000 copies per week), "to raise the thought of the Koreans and make them good subjects of the Empire." [37] It also published language books designed to teach Japanese to Korean laborers.[38]

Immigration restrictions were another important means of controlling Korean labor. During the early 1930's immigration was curtailed to ease the unemployment problem at home. After the North China incident of July, 1937,

[33] *Ibid.*, pp. 903–904.
[34] *Ibid.*, pp. 904–907.
[35] Naimushō keihokyoku hoanka, *Kyōwa jigyō kankei*, Reel 219, p. 90083. Hereafter cited as Kyōwakai, Reel 219.
[36] Kyōwakai, Reel 219, pp. 90042–90044.
[37] *Ibid.*, p. 90062.
[38] *Ibid.*, p. 90102. The Kyōwakai published 63,000 copies of a special textbook for immigrant laborers learning Japanese, and 5,000 volumes for the teachers.

regulations were designed to give the government more control over the number and quality of workers flowing into Japan. The government was concerned also with the danger of the illegal entry of Korean rebels.

After October 1, 1932, everyone in Korea was required to carry an identification card. Laborers who wanted to migrate to Japan had to prove that they had a job waiting for them.[39] Before the beginning of the Second World War, it was relatively easy for Korean students, businessmen, and others besides laborers to travel to Japan. When the war started, they also were restricted for security reasons.

In 1942 a comprehensive set of immigration regulations was applied to Korean laborers. The Koreans were to come as an organized group with the recommendation of the government-general and, whenever possible, were to enter Japan under the labor mobilization law. The old procedures of a police clearance and a crossing recommendation were continued.[40]

The home government, on March 18, 1942, also drew up a detailed agreement with the Korean government-general concerning Koreans coming to Japan:

Because of the war we must have tighter control of laborers. . . . Misunderstandings about working conditions . . . in Japan are to be cleared up before laborers leave for Japan. . . . General people coming do not need a special certificate but must present an identification card from a police station. . . . We must not allow dishonest Koreans into Japan. . . . You must pay special attention to the Korean people who are living in Japan and employ the smooth procedures of the Kyōwa Jigyō.[41]

[39] SUJ, 1933, pp. 1446–1447.
[40] *Ibid.*, 1942, p. 760.
[41] *Ibid.*, pp. 762–763.

The Role of Korean Labor in Japan's War Effort

The Korean labor force in Japan played an important role in Japan's war effort. Although there were labor disputes, no major incidents impaired war production. Hurriedly trained Koreans were perhaps less skillful than the Japanese they replaced in the factories and mines, but the central Kyōwakai maintained that trained Koreans were as good as Japanese laborers.[42]

Most "contract workers" (conscripted labor and volunteer labor) went to Japan to operate the coal and metal mines [43] so that Japanese laborers could be released for military service. The army had insisted that every Japanese male was a warrior first; consequently, the military conscription of coal miners continued until early 1945, regardless of the protests of mine operators.[44] The 1942 plan for national mobilization (kokumin dōin) called for a "more extensive use of Koreans . . . especially in mining and stevedoring."[45] By the end of March, 1943, 22 per cent of the miners in Hokkaido were Korean.[46] At the end of the war, the number of chōyōsha (requisitioned persons) in Japan was 680,000.[47]

The Koreans, like the rest of the Japanese labor force, were overworked during the last years of the war. It is a mistake, however, to apply the terms "slave labor" or

---

[42] Kyōwakai, Reel 219, p. 90087.

[43] Cohen, *Japan's Economy in War and Reconstruction*, p. 325. See also United States Strategic Bombing Survey, *The Effects of Strategic Bombing on Japan's War Economy*, p. 103. According to this source, the total number of Korean laborers brought into Japan from 1939 to 1945 was 667,684.

[44] Cohen, *Japan's Economy in War and Reconstruction*, p. 165.

[45] *Ibid.*, p. 314.

[46] "A War of Coal," *The Oriental Economist*, April, 1944, pp. 167–168.

[47] *Nihon kindaishi jiten*, p. 217. The Strategic Bombing Survey report cited in note 43 above gives a total of 667,684.

"forced labor battalions" to Korean workers.[48] They were no more mistreated, and in some cases were treated better, than their Japanese fellow workers, who were also conscripted. As the total mobilization program was stepped up, the entire labor force was put under great strain, and by the end of the war was quickly becoming exhausted.[49]

Many of the Korean laborers that came to Japan under the provisions of the Labor Mobilization Law were volunteers who signed two-year contracts and then returned to Korea. The number of disputes and the Japanese willingness to settle them in the workers' favor is further proof that Korean workers were not treated like slave laborers, as in Nazi Germany. In December, 1942, the government issued a set of regulations pertaining to Koreans whose two-year contracts were due to be completed. In this document the government directed lower officials to urge such Koreans to remain.[50] The use of force was not even suggested. The government had promised political equality, better working conditions, more pay, and other advantages to all Koreans. In short, the Korean laborers generally worked

[48] Many authors have applied these terms to the Korean minority in wartime Japan. For example, Jin Won Lee, "Brief Survey of Korean-Japanese Relations (Post-War Period)," *Koreana Quarterly*, I (Autumn, 1959), 65. Robert T. Oliver, *Verdict in Korea*, p. 175. Motoi Tamaki, "Nihon Kyōsantō no zainichi Chōsenjin shidō," *Koria Hyōron*, No. 38 (April, 1961), 26.

[49] Okochi, *Labor in Modern Japan*, p. 72.

[50] SUJ, 1942, p. 910. Kyōwakai, Reel 219, p. 90042. In April, 1944, *The Oriental Economist* published an article, "A War of Coal," complaining about the rapid turnover of Korean miners (italics mine): "About 50 per cent of the coal miners in Hokkaido are working men from Korea. In two years the Korean workers attain 80 per cent of Japanese efficiency, it is said. The trouble is that *their contracts usually run for only two years*. When the Korean miners . . . begin to develop efficiency, their term of contract expires. . . . In some cases they remain about six months after the expiry and produce at a rate of about 80 per cent, but after three years almost everyone of them leaves."

because of promised rewards and not because of threats.[51]

Koreans wanted to come to Japan until bombing began to make life difficult in Japanese cities. Before the raids, Koreans continued to be attracted by higher salaries and better opportunities. In 1942 the Home Ministry tried to stop the large number of Koreans who sought to enter Japan with no funds or jobs, but more kept coming each year.[52] The number of illegal entrants caught by the police rose to 7,400 in 1939, four times greater than in 1936.[53] Tighter immigration controls reduced this figure in 1941 to 4,705, but by 1942 it had increased slightly to 4,810.[54]

The official records contain no significant instances of anti-Japanese conduct or attempts by Koreans to sabotage the war effort. Police, Kyōwakai, and Home Ministry records indicate that most Koreans were obedient. A typical police report, probably compiled in late 1944, stated, "The majority of Koreans . . . are gradually accepting the actuality of Japanese-Korean harmony, and in the matter of increasing the production potential and in bearing arms, they are doing conspicuously well."[55]

Security and the Koreans

Although official reports comment favorably on the aid given by Koreans to the war effort, the government was not

---

[51] Cohen, *Japan's Economy in War and Reconstruction*, p. 326. Near the end of 1944 the Japanese need for labor grew so desperate that indirect methods of force were used to retain skilled laborers. "Those whose contracts had expired or were about to expire were 'advised' to stay another year. Those who did not take the advice but asked to return were told that unfortunately no shipping facilities were available." *Ibid.*

[52] SUJ, 1942, p. 763.
[53] *Ibid.*, 1939, p. 925.
[54] *Ibid.*, 1942, p. 772.
[55] *The Effects of Strategic Bombing on Japanese Morale*, p. 243.

always willing to entrust them with positions of responsibility. They were not eligible for military service before the Second World War. In April, 1942, it was decided at a cabinet conference to begin conscripting Koreans for the armed forces from 1944 onward.[56] Some Koreans expressed gratitude for this "gift" from the Emperor. Others felt that they should be granted certain rights before they began to die for the Empire in which they were not yet first-class citizens. They asked for enforcement of the compulsory education system, suffrage, equal rights, and abolition of crossing regulations.[57]

Japanese and Koreans wrote letters to the government about military service for Koreans. Out of 74 letters from Koreans, 11 thanked the government for conscription; 63 approved the plan but requested certain rights. Of 30 letters written by Japanese, one half said that the idea was good, and the other half thought it was too early to consider conscription of Koreans.[58]

In October, 1942, the Navy Ministry decided to use drafted Korean labor (rōmusha) for the first time. Only men that understood Japanese well and had no record of "dangerous thought" were to be taken. They had to be under thirty years of age, and single men were preferred. The ministry planned to draft 5,203 men. Using the facilities of the Kyōwakai, the Navy Ministry checked on the men before induction notices were distributed. Out of approximately 17,200 who received notices to report for an examination, over 7,000 failed to appear. Of the 9,816 who came for the examination, only 4,293 were inducted into service.[59] This

[56] SUJ, 1942, p. 857. The document gives no reason why 1944 was chosen.
[57] *Ibid.*, p. 858.
[58] *Ibid.*, pp. 858–870.
[59] *Ibid.*, pp. 871–873.

poor response discouraged the Japanese from giving Koreans positions of greater trust.

It was in the management of the Kyōwakai that the Japanese showed how little they trusted the Koreans in Japan. Welfare Ministry Regulation 145, of December 26, 1942, stated that the leaders of the Kyōwakai had to be Koreans. But on this crucial issue the Welfare Ministry was overruled by the police bureau of the Home Ministry. The police bureau pointed out that the leaders of the Kyōwakai had to work closely with the police stations and to handle classified information that must not fall into Korean hands. The bureau insisted that only Japanese be chosen.[60] As a result, the Kyōwakai, primarily an association for Koreans, was run by Japanese officials.

The War's End

As the bombing became heavier, the hostility between Japanese and Koreans was more openly expressed. The Japanese tended to use the Koreans as scapegoats. According to police records, "after one great air raid, rumors among Japanese concerning the Koreans increased twofold as compared with the day before the attack, whereas rumors among the Koreans concerning the Japanese increased approximately two and one-half times." [61] Japanese rumors said that "the Koreans aided and abetted enemy strategy and that they fled in the face of enemy action." [62] Late in the war a rumor circulated throughout northern Kyushu that Koreans wearing white clothing (the traditional Korean costume) went into the mountains during air raids to direct enemy planes

---

[60] Naimushō keihokyoku hoanka, *Kyōwakai kankei kaigi shorui shōgakukai kankei o fukumu*, p. 87060.
[61] *Ibid.*, p. 250.
[62] *Ibid.*

to their targets.[63] The Koreans spread rumors that a volunteer army of Korean immigrants to the United States was advancing on Japan. A Korean woman started a widespread rumor that, "should enemy paratroopers come, they might kill the Japanese but would probably spare the Koreans." [64]

As the war neared its end, thousands of Koreans began to return to the peninsula until, after August, 1945, this movement swelled into a mass exodus. Nevertheless, at the war's end a large Korean minority remained in Japan. Their legal status was unclear, and it was left to the American occupation government to decide their future.

---

[63] Personal interview with Mrs. Yukiko Blaschko, April 16, 1963, Madison, Wisconsin.

[64] *The Effects of Strategic Bombing on Japanese Morale*, p. 250.

VII
PROBLEMS OF ASSIMILATION

Until 1945 the Japanese government maintained a policy of assimilating the Koreans.[1] This official policy, however, was severely circumscribed by the nature of a Japanese society which was hostile to the absorption of aliens, especially Koreans. The Japanese social system, with its emphasis upon the family and the group, had no place for the migrants. Individuals had no identity independent of these social units, and within this traditional system each person occupied "his prescribed, recognized and respected place."[2] Furthermore, the Japanese were extremely con-

---

[1] A suitable interpretation of the word "assimilation" has been set forth by Inis L. Claude: "Assimilation demands that minorities consent to abandon the ethnic, cultural, and linguistic characteristics which distinguish them from the national majorities with whom they live, and to become merged into nationally uniform communities with the majorities." *National Minorities*, p. 79.

[2] Jean Stoetzel, *Without the Chrysanthemum and the Sword*, p. 56. Robert N. Bellah, *Tokugawa Religion*, p. 13.

scious of their "uniqueness" as Japanese.[3] Koreans who migrated to Japan, at least for the first generation, were unable to penetrate this tightly structured society.

This conservative social structure was not peculiar to the Japanese countryside but also extended into the cities where the majority of migrant Koreans settled. Instead of growing weaker in the urban environment, the family and the group, and the personal ties that facilitated social intercourse grew stronger. It has been suggested that "the rapidity of changes in other spheres tended to create a greater dependence on the family."[4] Traditional values were also maintained among those employed in small urban factories and businesses.[5]

If a distinction is made between assimilation as an official policy and assimilation as an informal social process, it is easy to see that there was a direct conflict between the formal and the informal, and that Japanese society sabotaged Japan's own assimilation policy. Japanese discrimination, combined with Korean unwillingness to become Japanized, severely limited the success of the assimilation process, and despite many examples of cooperation, animosity between the two peoples seems to have increased.

The Japanese considered the Koreans an inferior people. A Home Ministry report of 1933 noted that most of the Koreans immigrating to Japan were low-class tenant farmers or unskilled laborers, illiterate in both Japanese and Korean, and that only a few of them spoke Japanese. "Almost all of them," it stated, "are very wild and deeply emotional; and as a result, they like to argue and fight." The

[3] Robert N. Bellah, "Japan's Cultural Identity," *The Journal of Asian Studies*, XXIV (August, 1965), 573.
[4] John K. Fairbank, Edwin O. Reischauer, and Albert M. Craig, *East Asia the Modern Transformation*, p. 523.
[5] *Ibid.*, 524.

report stressed the increase in "bad habits and vices" of the Koreans and the consequent increased crime rate. It concluded that the Koreans were "scorned" (shidan) by the Japanese.[6] Every Home Ministry annual report from the earliest one until the last, issued in 1942, contains similar statements. The Japanese view of the Koreans grew even blacker after 1939, when the provisions of the Labor Mobilization Law went into effect and thousands of Korean laborers came to Japan.

A large number of disputes between the two peoples were annually reported to the police, despite the assimilation efforts of the centralized Kyōwakai and the tightened police controls of the war years.[7]

Year	No. of disputes	Year	No. of disputes
1933	6,525	1938	1,712
1935	3,461	1939	1,767
1936	2,929	1942	734

These disputes were caused by drunkenness, ethnic differences, financial problems, mistakes at work, and "foolish love" (shijō). Although the number of disputes decreased during the war years, the percentage of quarrels caused by ethnic differences rose. In 1938 only 28 (approximately one-sixtieth) of the disputes were the result of ethnic differences. By 1942 the percentage of ethnic disputes had risen to about one-third of the total.[8]

As the immigrant contract laborers began to enter Japan after 1939, the number of Koreans involved in labor disputes also rose sharply after a period of decline.[9]

[6] SUJ, 1933, p. 1401.
[7] These figures do not include labor disputes and criminal statistics. SUJ, 1933, p. 1616; 1936, p. 1527; 1939, p. 1017; 1942, pp. 925–926.
[8] *Ibid.*, 1942, p. 926.
[9] *Ibid.*, 1939, p. 1022; 1942, p. 929.

Year	No. of labor disputes	No. of Koreans involved
1938	168	3,685
1939	153	9,630
1941	96	4,977
1942	172	8,499

Disputes over rented housing reached a high of 5,504 in 1933 and then began to drop rapidly near the end of the decade. By 1942 there were only 99 incidents involving 176 people.[10] The government attributed the decrease in all types of disputes, except ones about labor, to the Kyōwakai, but the Japanese police probably deserve the credit.

The degree of Japanese official discrimination against the Koreans gradually changed during the 1930's and early 1940's. As the war crisis deepened, the granting of full citizenship to Koreans was again discussed in high places. The Emperor formally announced that all his subjects in Japan and Korea were equal in every way.[11] In reality, however, few Koreans in the peninsula gained full equality as Japanese citizens. Koreans in Japan were in a more favorable position, but even they had attained only semi-citizen status. Koreans were sometimes paid less than Japanese, barred from certain Japanese schools, and forbidden to serve in the military. The Korean government-general was aware of this discrimination and, in a report to the Home Ministry in 1939, officially requested that some abuses be stopped.[12]

Much of the anti-Japanese agitation by students and intellectuals may probably be ascribed to Japanese discrimination against Koreans in general. Discrimination, combined

---

[10] *Ibid.*, 1933, p. 1638; 1942, p. 933.
[11] Edward W. Wagner, *The Korean Minority in Japan*, pp. 36–37.
[12] SUJ, 1939, pp. 922–923. Among other things the government-general requested policemen to be more polite.

with traditional hatred, helps to explain the "biased nationalistic point of view" held by the Korean population.[13] As for the Koreans who became communists, there was a clear connection between discrimination from the Japanese and Korean membership in the Japanese Communist Party. The Japanese police interrogated all arrested members of the Japanese Communist Party, asking each person why he became a communist. The answers given by the Koreans are revealing. They became communists, they said, because the independence of Korea could not be realized otherwise; because they wanted racial freedom; because of unemployment; and because, after they came to Japan, they received discriminatory treatment and felt antipathy toward the Japanese. The police report noted that the reasons given by Koreans were basically different from those of the Japanese who were members of the Communist Party.[14]

Politics and the Kyōwakai might have been used to draw the two peoples closer together. The Japanese, however, failed to use the former properly, and grossly distorted the original purpose of the latter, rendering it useless as a tool for assimilation by excluding Koreans from positions of leadership. Some Koreans found an outlet for their talents in public life. The first Korean attempt to enter politics was in January, 1929, when a Korean in Sakai became an unsuccessful candidate for a municipal office. In February, 1932, Pak Ch'un-gŭm (Pak Shun-kin) ran for the Diet and won.[15] Thereafter, Korean interest in politics grew rapidly. Twenty-seven Korean candidates entered political races held at all levels in 1933, and eight were elected. The Ko-

[13] *Ibid.*, 1933, p. 1397.
[14] *Ibid.*, pp. 1457–1458.
[15] SUJ, 1936, p. 1497. Pak won again in 1936 but lost in 1942. *Ibid.*, 1942, p. 876. Pak was one of the founders of the Sōaikai. Yu-gan Yi, *A Fifty-Year History of the Koreans in Japan*, p. 85.

Problems of Assimilation

rean candidates were concerned primarily with the housing problem, the immigration problem, and abolition of racial discrimination. During the campaigns, the Korean politicians spoke of peace between Koreans and Japanese and tried to capture the Japanese vote.[16] Between 1929 and 1939 there were 187 Korean candidates for public office; 53 of them were elected.[17] Korean candidates usually ran for office in areas heavily populated by Koreans.

Assimilation might have been aided if the Japanese government had encouraged Koreans to take a more active part in local and national elections, and if the 1925 election law had been modified to fit Koreans.[18] Although some Koreans were eligible to vote, few were interested in doing so. In 1936 the government made a study of ten districts where 41,829 Koreans were eligible to vote, but 67.4 per cent did not go to the polls, while the Japanese rate for the same districts was 23.8 per cent.[19] In 1939 the number of Koreans eligible to vote was large enough to induce Japanese politicians to print handbills in Korean for distribution in Korean districts. They also selected Koreans to serve on their election committees.[20] By 1942, Koreans that could vote began to show more interest in elections, and the abstention rate dropped to between 20 and 40 per cent.[21] The Japanese

[16] SUJ, 1936, p. 1497.
[17] *Ibid.*, 1939, p. 985.
[18] Korean males over twenty-five living in Japan were enfranchised by the election law of May 5, 1925. The law, however, contained many restrictions that severely limited their participation. The law required a voter to live in one place for more than a year without interruption; recipients of public or private relief were not eligible and; each voter had to write the names of the candidates on the ballot in Japanese. (This last requirement was eventually removed.)
[19] SUJ, 1936, p. 1499.
[20] *Ibid.*, 1939, pp. 984–985.
[21] *Ibid.*, 1942, p. 876.

government attributed this result to the activities of the Kyōwakai.

Although the original peace and friendship groups had been established mainly to help the newly arrived Koreans with social problems and to assimilate them, the Kyōwakai now became nothing more than an arm of the Japanese police. The idea behind the original Kyōwakai, before the war, was equality and harmony. After 1939, however, the Japanese distorted the original purpose of the organization by occupying all of the important positions. By 1942 all the subgroups were headed by the local police chiefs, and the officials under them were members of the Special Higher Police.[22] No doubt the Kyōwakai did pressure the Koreans to support the war, but in the process the Japanese destroyed the original foundation upon which the organization had been built.

Perhaps one of the greatest hindrances to assimilation was the difficulty in communication between the Korean laborers and the Japanese. At the end of 1936 the government checked 616,779 Koreans (there were 690,501 in Japan) and found that 342,988, or 55 per cent, were illiterate in both Korean and Japanese. If the number of young people who were required to be in grade school, but were not, is included in the total, it becomes 61 per cent. The government also discovered that 31 per cent of the Koreans understood no spoken Japanese.[23] In 1942 the government made another extensive survey and checked 1,404,848 Koreans out of a total of 1,625,054 in Japan, with these results: 60 per cent were illiterate in both Japanese and Korean, and 29 per cent did not understand spoken Japanese.[24]

The Kyōwakai made a great effort to teach basic Japanese

[22] *Ibid.*, 1942, p. 921.
[23] *Ibid.*, 1936, p. 1376.
[24] *Ibid.*, 1942, p. 742.

	1936	*1942*
Understand very well	187,583	504,890
Understand a little	233,647	521,921
Understand not at all	196,549	385,511

to newly arrived Korean laborers, but during the war years they came too fast for this program to be effective. In addition, many laborers returned to Korea after their two-year contract expired.

Judging by their public statements, the Japanese did not seem to recognize the magnitude of the problem of the assimilation of Koreans. "It is expected," wrote a Japanese scholar in 1937, "that, in the long run, they will be absorbed into the Japanese blood, as has been the case in Japanese history from time immemorial." [25] General Minami Jirō, the governor-general of Korea, noted the striking progress made in the assimilation of the Koreans by 1939.[26] Home Ministry reports, however, were less enthusiastic. In the same year, a report stated that true assimilation was still far away.[27]

The Japanese government was now beginning to realize that assimilation of the Koreans was going to be a long and arduous task that would require more than official pronouncements. The government discarded some of its former ideas and began to work actively toward its goal by creating a central Kyōwakai in 1939.

It is extremely difficult to determine the success or failure of assimilation among the Koreans in Japan. In the first place, large numbers of Koreans had been living in Japan

---

[25] Ryoichi Ishii, *Population Pressure and Economic Life in Japan*, p. 208.

[26] Jiro Minami, "Japanese-Korean 'Fusion' Said Vital to Creation of New Order in East Asia," *The China Weekly Review*, August 19, 1939, p. 379.

[27] SUJ, 1939, p. 888.

for only 25 years when Japan suffered defeat in 1945. This relatively short span of time, roughly half an average lifetime, was hardly enough to allow Japanese official policies to take full effect. It seems fair to say, however, that from the official point of view the assimilation policy was partially successful. The Koreans in Japan did support the war effort, and a considerable number of them decided to remain in Japan after the end of the war. Linguistic evidence also suggests that many were partially assimilated. The movement of great numbers of laborers in and out of Japan during the wartime period further clouds the issue and makes it difficult to reach a conclusion. Among these laborers, assimilation worked badly, if at all. The basic prerequisite for assimilation was teaching Japanese to the Koreans, and the Japanese were unable to accomplish this fully. Hence they could not change the ethnic and cultural patterns of the Koreans. To this basic failure must be added the Japanese prejudice against the Koreans and the Korean's long tradition of hatred for the Japanese. The growth of a new Korean nationalism during the 1920's and 1930's also worked against assimilation. Many of the Koreans in Japan, products of a culture with a longer historical continuity than that of the Japanese, had no desire to abandon the characteristics which distinguished them from the Japanese. Perhaps even more important was the very nature of a Japanese society which had no place for Koreans. Japanese particularism proved stronger than the universalistic doctrine of assimilation.[28]

One final though important barrier to assimilation should be considered. Korean migrants tended to settle near earlier arrivals, and this resulted in Korean settlements within Japanese communities. The cause was as much Ko-

[28] Bellah, "Japan's Cultural Identity," 573–594.

rean desire to settle together as Japanese discrimination against their Korean neighbors. The new arrivals, often speaking no Japanese, sought aid from other countrymen in finding jobs and places to live. This isolated existence separated the Koreans from the main flow of Japanese life and further retarded the assimilation process.

VIII

THE KOREAN MINORITY IN OCCUPIED JAPAN, 1945–1952

Defeat in the Second World War destroyed the Japanese Empire, but the problem of the Korean minority—a problem spawned by that empire—remained. The American military government in Japan inherited this complex situation, which for decades had defied correction by the old imperial government. The basic issue facing the Supreme Commander for the Allied Powers (SCAP) was the status of the Koreans in Japan during the American occupation.

From the beginning of the occupation the Japanese and the Koreans found no mutually acceptable solution. When SCAP decreed that Koreans were to be treated as "Japanese nationals" for administrative purposes during the occupation period, the Koreans demanded that they be given the same status as other members of the United Nations in Japan. After nearly four decades of Japanese rule, they still rejected the classification "Japanese nationals." SCAP used the Japanese government in an effort to force the Koreans to accept it, but the Koreans refused to do so peaceably.

Relations between Japanese and Koreans were similar to those before the war in some respects and different in others. The traditional hostility continued, but there was a new note of bitterness resulting from Japan's defeat. The Korean and Japanese communists again joined forces as they had done in the late 1920's and early 1930's in a bid to overthrow the conservative Japanese government, ruling under SCAP's guidance. The Korean communists continued to put nationalism first. New elements such as the presence of SCAP, the division of the peninsula into two states, and the division of most of the world into two power blocs lifted the problem of the Korean minority from a national issue to one of international significance.

SCAP's primary concern was the disarmament and democratization of the Japanese. As the Korean movement in Japan became increasingly involved in the Japanese and international communist movements, SCAP began to regard the Koreans in Japan as an obstacle to its reform program for the Japanese. Its position was similar to that of the old imperial Japanese government, and it came to regard the Korean communist movement as subversive. SCAP also reacted in a manner similar to that of the old imperial government by suppressing the Korean organizations that interfered with its program.

Repatriation

Months before the final defeat of Japan, the Koreans began to return home. Thousands of them, profiting from the confusion of the spring and summer of 1945, simply walked away from the factories and the mines.

At first the defeated Japanese government adopted a conciliatory attitude toward the Koreans returning to the peninsula and to those who remained in Japan. On the day before surrender, August 14, 1945, the chief of the Special Higher Police sent a special order, "Emergency Measures for the Korean People," to every police station in Japan. To prevent friction between Koreans and Japanese, the police were to protect the lives and property of all Koreans. Whenever possible, the two peoples were to be kept apart, and leaders in both communities were to be cautioned not to cause trouble.[1]

At the end of the war there were approximately 2,400,000 Koreans living in Japan.[2] The United States government had long been aware of the problems of this minority group. The occupation forces that entered Japan, however, came with no concrete plans for the Koreans in Japan, for it was expected that the Koreans would solve the problem by returning to Korea.

For three months after the surrender, the repatriation of Koreans continued, as usual, without government supervision. The Koreans were free to leave Japan whenever they could obtain passage across the Korea strait. There were no restrictions on the amount of currency or goods they could take with them. From August 15 to November 30, 1945, approximately 800,000 returned.[3]

The first important SCAP directive dealing with Korean repatriation was published on November 1, 1945. The Koreans in Japan were offered free transportation back to Korea, but were permitted to take only 1,000 yen in cash, worth 20 packages of cigarettes, and the baggage they could carry with them. The currency limitation remained in force

---

[1] Naimushō keihokyoku hoanka, *Nendobetsu Chōsenjin* . . . , pp. 93676–93677.
[2] *Nihon kindaishi jiten*, p. 217.
[3] Edward W. Wagner, *The Korean Minority in Japan*, p. 43.

throughout the entire repatriation period, but the baggage allowance was soon increased. Later, Koreans were allowed to take bank and postal savings books, insurance policies, and other negotiable documents. These concessions meant little, however, for all financial transactions between Korea and Japan were prohibited. The official repatriation program ended on December 31, 1946, but before this date all Koreans in Japan had been given the opportunity to return to Korea and an additional 575,000 Koreans returned to their homeland.[4]

Although the official repatriation program had ended, SCAP and the Japanese government were happy to allow another 15,000 Koreans to return to Korea after this date. By August, 1947, the repatriation was over. Most Koreans who remained in Japan after this date had forfeited their right to be repatriated.[5]

Well over one-fifth of the Koreans in Japan at the end of the Second World War had elected to remain. The policies imposed by SCAP for regulating the amount of money and personal effects to be taken into Korea probably encouraged some Koreans to remain in Japan. This is, however, only one of several possible reasons for them to remain. Korea rapidly fell into a state of economic collapse after the war ended. The Koreans in Japan heard about the difficult economic conditions, and many hesitated to return. Reports filtered back to Japan of floods and epidemics in the southern part of Korea, the section from which most of the Koreans in Japan had come. It was learned also that the Koreans who had remained at home resented those who

[4] *Ibid.*, pp. 44–46. All the Koreans discussed here went to the American zone south of the 38th parallel; 351 elected to go to the Soviet zone and were repatriated in a separate agreement. *Ibid.*, p. 49.
[5] *Ibid.*, p. 48.

were returning.[6] Of the 600,000 that remained in Japan after 1948, 300,000 to 400,000 had immigrated to Japan before 1930 and had settled there permanently.[7]

Ironically, SCAP helped to perpetuate the problem by its tight regulation of the repatriation program. At first, as hundreds of thousands of Koreans poured back into Korea, it seemed that all of them would be gone within a few months. SCAP decided, however, to end the unregulated movement, which, it was feared, might cause the spread of disease and facilitate a black market in Japanese currency. Moreover, SCAP needed the ships used to transport the Koreans.

Korean Organizations

After August 15, 1945, Korean associations began to appear in many parts of Japan. The Zainichi Chōsenjin Renmei, called Chōren (League of Koreans in Japan), because of its apt and forceful leadership, soon became the outstanding Korean organization in Japan. Chōren established its central headquarters in Tokyo and had branch offices in every prefecture and city where Koreans lived.[8]

Chōren was officially organized to deal with repatriation, conflicts between Koreans and Japanese, and economic aid for needy Koreans. In reality it engaged in many other activities and, during the first few confused months of the occupation, functioned as a quasi-governmental organization in its dealings with the Japanese. As pressure was ex-

[6] Jin Won Lee, "Brief Survey of Korean-Japanese Relations (Post-War Period)," *Koreana Quarterly*, I (Autumn, 1959), 49.

[7] Kwang chul Rim, "Problem of the Koreans in Japan," *Contemporary Japan*, XXII (1953), 328.

[8] Public Security Investigation Agency, *Current Phases of the Activities of Korean Residents in Japan*, p. 1. Wagner, *The Korean Minority in Japan*, pp. 51–52. "Koreans in Japan (1)," *Korea Journal*, II (April, 1962), 50–51.

erted on the Japanese government to meet the demands of Chōren, the organization steadily grew more powerful.

In the first confused months after Japan's surrender, the Japanese government hesitated to act, and the American military government was not yet in full operation. During this period, Chōren was able to seize control of the repatriation program. The Japanese Ministry of Transportation and owners of larger private ships were induced to put shipping at its disposal, and Chōren representatives worked with Japanese officials in scheduling special trains to bring Koreans to ports of embarkation.[9] In November, SCAP officially assumed control of the repatriation of Koreans, but the Japanese government continued to allow Chōren to select the people to fill the daily quotas for repatriation. This privilege gave Chōren great strength. In May, 1946, SCAP directed that this practice be abolished.

In dealing with the Japanese and SCAP, Chōren often acted as though it held sovereign power over all the Koreans in Japan as well as those repatriated. It carried on a large welfare program, using supplies received from the Japanese Welfare Ministry; it dispensed justice to Korean criminals turned over by the Japanese police; and it promoted educational programs. To gain office space, Chōren moved into large buildings in Tokyo and Osaka that formerly had been connected with the government-general of Korea. Funds to finance Chōren's many activities were raised in several ways. Chōren kept the bank and postal savings books of repatriates and, by direct negotiation with the Ministry of Finance, managed to obtain more than 100,000,000 yen during the first four months of 1946. Chōren also approached Japanese firms which had previously employed Koreans and exerted pressure on them to pay "back wages" and "separation bonuses." Most of this money was kept by Chōren. Another

---

[9] Wagner, *The Korean Minority in Japan*, p. 51.

means of obtaining funds was through black-market operations.[10]

Chōren, originally organized by Koreans with diverse political aims, soon fell under the control of Korean communists who had reactivated their prewar cooperation with the Japanese Communist Party. The front man and chairman for Chōren was Yun Keun, a Christian minister and political moderate.[11] But the real power was held by Kim Ch'ŏn-hae (Kin Ten-kai). Kim, a veteran communist leader who had spent most of the 1930's and the entire wartime period in prison, was released in October, 1945, after Japan's defeat. He was now a member of the Politburo of the Japanese Communist Party and the leader of Chōren. From 1945 until the fall of 1949 Kim fulfilled a twofold mission. He was an unofficial ambassador of the communist regime in North Korea at the Japan Communist Party headquarters in Tokyo, and he coordinated the movements of Koreans in Japan with the activities of the Japanese Communist Party.[12]

Chōren's rapid turn toward the radical left caused a split within the organization before the end of 1945. The Shin Chōsen Kensetsusha Dōmei (League of Founders of the New Korea), a right-wing group including former Chōren members and new members, was established in October, 1946, with Pak Yŏl as its first leader.[13] This organization developed into the Zainichi Daikanminkoku Kyoryūmindan (Community of Korean Residents in Japan), known

[10] *Ibid.*, pp. 52–53.
[11] *Ibid.*, p. 54.
[12] Rodger Swearingen and Paul Langer, *Red Flag in Japan*, p. 123.
[13] *Current Phases* . . . , p. 19. "Koreans in Japan (2)," *Korea Journal*, II (May, 1962), 50. Another splinter group was created as a result of Chōren's rapid movement toward the left: Chōsen Kenkoku Sokushin Seinen Dōmei (Korean Youth League to Promote the Construction of the State), abbreviated Kensei. This anticommunist group of young men, founded in November, 1945, was eventually absorbed by

as Mindan, in August, 1948. Mindan maintained connections with the Republic of Korea and quickly became the arch rival of Chōren. The division of Korea into north and south, communist and noncommunist, was reflected in the political ideology of the Koreans in Japan. From then until the present, left-wing and right-wing Korean groups in Japan have been bitter enemies. The few Koreans who refused to join either wing had little influence.

The Legal Status of Koreans in Japan

From the beginning of the occupation, SCAP had planned to treat the Koreans as a liberated people. As one observer wrote, "Implicit in the Occupation's democratization program was the emancipation of the Koreans from the oppressive and discriminatory controls under which they had lived."[14] SCAP, however, was concerned primarily with the disarmament and democratization of Japan and not with the problems of the minority group. Even after its early attitude of sympathy and its implicit concern for the welfare of the Koreans, SCAP gave the minority no preferential position in relation to the Japanese in occupied Japan. Early in the occupation, SCAP informed the Japanese government that it expected the Koreans to be regulated by the same laws and to be treated in the same manner as the defeated Japanese.[15]

In an attempt to clarify the legal status of the Koreans who remained unrepatriated, SCAP issued a decree on November 20, 1946, that any Korean who refused repatria-

Mindan in 1950. Before this occurred, however, Kensei members were involved in many bloody fights with Chōren. Kensei membership never rose above 20,000. Yu-gan Yi, *A Fifty-Year History of the Koreans in Japan*, pp. 123–125.

[14] Wagner, *The Korean Minority in Japan*, p. 41.

[15] Heiji Shinozaki, *Zainichi Chōsenjin undō* (The Korean movement in Japan), p. 14.

tion automatically fell under the jurisdiction of Japanese law and would be treated as a Japanese. The Koreans, the Japanese, and SCAP all had anticipated that the peace treaty with Japan would clarify the status of the minority. Even after SCAP's pronouncement, the position of the Koreans in Japan remained uncertain for the duration of the occupation.[16]

In criminal matters the Japanese government had complete jurisdiction over the Koreans. Unlike the Japanese, however, Koreans could appeal to SCAP for a retrial.[17] Unless the Koreans in Japan elected to become Japanese citizens, they were not eligible to vote in Japanese elections,[18] but they had to pay the same taxes the Japanese paid.[19] Koreans were officially given the same food rations as the Japanese.[20] In economic activities, Koreans were supposed to be treated exactly like Japanese unless they had come to Japan after September 2, 1945, in which case they were to be treated like other foreigners.[21]

On January 24, 1948, the Education Ministry announced that Korean schools must follow the program outlined by Japanese law. The Koreans were told to teach in Japanese and to use Japanese textbooks.[22]

The Japanese Anti-Korean Campaign

Relations between Japanese and Koreans rapidly deteriorated after the end of the war. Many Koreans, bitter after

[16] *Ibid.*
[17] *Ibid.*, p. 17. The right of appeal was limited to the more important cases.
[18] *Ibid.*, p. 18.
[19] *Ibid.*, p. 19.
[20] *Ibid.*, p. 20.
[21] *Ibid.*, p. 21.
[22] *Ibid.*, pp. 21–22.

the long years of subordination under Japanese rule, resented the fact that their legal status had been equated with that of the Japanese. They wished to be treated as a liberated people, as members of the community of the victorious Allied Powers, which officially would give them a higher status than the Japanese. Many Koreans thought of themselves as slaves freed by Japan's defeat. In 1945 a Korean publication described their attitude in this naïve but graphic manner: "We are second-class people but the Japanese are fourth class. Therefore, we naturally are going to receive much better treatment and the Japanese worse." [23]

During the early days of the occupation, the Japanese government, uncertain of its position in regard to the Koreans in Japan and unsure of SCAP policy, was circumspect in its dealings with the minority group; but, as the initial shock of defeat wore off, the Japanese launched a nation-wide attack on the Koreans. In less than a year after the end of the war, the Koreans were again made the national scapegoat and came under direct attack by the press, the Diet, and various branches of the Japanese government, which, with the tacit approval of SCAP, slandered them and discriminated against them. The Koreans were accused of creating Japan's black market, of increasing the crime rate, of being carriers of disease, of not paying taxes, of having secured a financial stranglehold on Japan, and of being brave only after the war was over.[24]

On July 13, 1946, the *Tokyo Mainichi* attacked the Koreans for their black-market operations and pointed out that the Japanese police had a right to regulate such activities. Just six days later the police tested their authority in a clash near Shibuya Station in Tokyo where five persons

[23] *Ibid.*, p. 195.
[24] David Conde, "The Korean Minority in Japan," *Far Eastern Survey*, XVI (February, 1947), 41.

were killed and many black-market operators were arrested.[25]

The general secretary of the Liberal Party, Ono Tomemutsu, denounced the non-Japanese who, he said, were destroying the social order.[26] Two weeks later Finance Minister Ishibashi Tanzan gave credibility to another anti-Korean rumor when he noted that "third-party nationals" controlled twenty of the fifty billion yen in circulation.[27] On August 17 a violently anti-Korean speech was delivered on the floor of the Diet by Shiikuma Saburō. In his speech, reportedly written in the Home Ministry, Shiikuma stated, "We refuse to stand by in silence watching Formosans and Koreans, who have resided in Japan as Japanese up to the time of surrender, swaggering about as if they were nationals of victorious nations. . . . The actions of these Koreans and Formosans makes the blood in our veins, in our misery of defeat, boil." He also accused Koreans of being the nucleus of the black market and asserted that they controlled one-third of the new yen in circulation.[28]

Early in November, 1946, the police posted hundreds of anti-Korean posters on walls throughout the Ueno area of Tokyo. On a poster warning people to beware of robbers, a Korean emblem was used as a background against which a robber, armed with a knife, threatened a trembling woman.[29]

SCAP contributed to the anti-Korean hysteria by issuing a press release from headquarters expressing fear that Koreans illegally entering Japan were spreading cholera and

[25] *Ibid.*, pp. 41–42. The Japanese police were specifically charged by SCAP to maintain order. Wagner, *The Korean Minority in Japan*, p. 59.
[26] Conde, "The Korean Minority in Japan," p. 42.
[27] *Ibid.*
[28] *Ibid.*, p. 43.
[29] *Ibid.*, p. 45.

The Korean Minority in Occupied Japan

typhus. It was not until nearly two months later that SCAP withdrew this charge and admitted that only one case of cholera had developed.[30] SCAP cannot be excused from responsibility in the anti-Korean hysteria that swept Japan during the summer and fall of 1946. SCAP censors had to authorize all attacks on Koreans that appeared in the Japanese press. SCAP itself expressed anti-Korean sentiments, and many of its members did not conceal their pro-Japanese feelings.[31]

Many Koreans did engage in black-market activities, as did nearly everyone in Japan. The economy was shattered at the end of the war, and it was necessary to buy and sell on the black market to obtain enough food to live. The black market was nothing new to the Japanese; it had flourished throughout the war.[32] In fact, Prince Higashikuni Naruhiko, Japan's first postwar premier, stated that the enormous extent of black-market activity during the war had helped defeat Japan.[33]

Major Incidents

SCAP and the Japanese government decided that Koreans who had not been repatriated were subject to Japanese jurisdiction until their status could be determined by the conclusion of a peace treaty. The Koreans resented their subservient status and many demanded retribution for the way in which they had been treated by the Japanese. It was almost inevitable that this explosive situation should produce trouble.

Almost immediately after hostilities ceased, unrepatriated

---

[30] *Ibid.*, p. 43.
[31] *Ibid.*, p. 45.
[32] United States Strategic Bombing Survey, *The Effects of Strategic Bombing on Japanese Morale*, p. 17.
[33] Conde, "The Korean Minority in Japan," p. 43.

Korean coal miners rioted, and SCAP was forced to dispatch troops to restore order. In the cities, fights often broke out between angry Koreans and Japanese police. SCAP, whose main aim was to preserve order while carrying out its program for Japan, lost much of its earlier sympathy for the minority and urged the Japanese authorities to take stronger action in controlling the Koreans.

Both SCAP and the Japanese government were concerned about illegal entry of Koreans into Japan and the black-market activity of those already there. In an effort to solve both problems, the Japanese authorities in Osaka, in late 1946, ordered all Koreans in that city to submit to a special registration. Every Korean was to carry an identification card, with his picture and fingerprints, at all times. When the Koreans refused to comply with the government order, the registration in Osaka could not be carried out.[34]

Acting on a suggestion from SCAP, the Japanese government proclaimed an alien registration order on May 2, 1947.[35] The Koreans, who for most purposes were considered Japanese nationals, were classified as aliens for the purposes of registration. One scholar has justified the procedure by saying that a registration of aliens was badly needed for "administration and control purposes." He also pointed out that the registration was not discriminatory, since all foreigners except occupation personnel were expected to register.[36] The Koreans, however, felt that the registration was aimed at them. Faced by what they considered a serious threat to their existence in Japan, the Korean organizations united in opposition and encouraged their members not to register. They presented five major objections to the law:

[34] Wagner, *The Korean Minority in Japan*, p. 66.
[35] *Korea Journal*, II (May, 1962), p. 49.
[36] Wagner, *The Korean Minority in Japan*, p. 66.

The Korean Minority in Occupied Japan

(1) The registration was not based on established international procedures.

(2) It should be conducted by the various Korean organizations, not by the Japanese government.

(3) Koreans should be accorded full and continuous treatment as foreign nationals, and not receive such treatment merely for the purpose of the registration.

(4) The lives and properties of Koreans in Japan should be properly safeguarded.

(5) The Japanese government should take steps to insure that the Japanese people know and respect the status of Koreans.[37]

At the end of the month-long registration period few Koreans had registered. SCAP, realizing it was impossible to arrest and prosecute all Koreans in Japan, extended the deadline another month. When the Koreans still refused to register, SCAP published an announcement "emphasizing that the purpose of the registration was to protect, not restrict, the rights of minority groups." By combining this concession with further threats, SCAP at last persuaded the Koreans to comply.[38]

The dispute over Korean registration was mild compared to the incidents that arose when SCAP and the Japanese government attempted to control the Korean system of education. Soon after the occupation of Japan, Korean organizations began to establish a separate school system for Korean children. Classes were conducted in Korean and were designed to give a Korean rather than a Japanese education. Chōren was especially active in establishing Korean schools, and by the end of September, 1946, it had established 525 schools throughout Japan. Thirteen months

[37] *Ibid.*, p. 67.
[38] *Ibid.*

later the number of schools had increased to 578 with about 62,000 students and 1,500 teachers.[39]

It was not until October, 1947, more than two years after the beginning of the occupation, that SCAP took official notice of the autonomous Korean school system. SCAP then suggested that the Japanese government check to see whether the Korean schools were following all the directives of the Japanese Ministry of Education.[40] The Japanese Ministry of Education complied by issuing a directive to prefectural governors that Japanese standards must be enforced in Korean schools.[41]

The Koreans realized that this directive would mean that many Korean schools would be closed because the teachers and equipment of many of them could not meet the standards of Japanese law. Also, Koreans had induced the Japanese to allow part-time use of school buildings, and these would have to be vacated if the law were obeyed.

Chōren led the fight to maintain an autonomous Korean education system, but its appeals to SCAP went unanswered. In April, 1948, the Japanese began to enforce the directive and closed unaccredited Korean schools. Japanese police met resistance in all parts of Japan as they closed Korean schools, but the most spectacular clash occurred in Kobe. Here, because of extreme recalcitrance on both sides, the

[39] Mindan controlled about forty schools. *Ibid.*, p. 68. The total number of Mindan students was only 6,828. Yi, *A Fifty-Year History of the Koreans in Japan*, p. 166. The Chōren-affiliated schools indoctrinated their students with communist philosophy and encouraged patriotic feeling toward the homeland. *Ibid.*

[40] Wagner, *The Korean Minority in Japan*, p. 69. The Korean schools were permitted to teach the Korean language as an addition to the curriculum.

[41] Shinozaki, *Zainichi Chōsenjin undō*, p. 21. The Ministry of Education did concede, however, that the Korean language could be taught as an extra subject outside regular classes. Yi, *A Fifty-Year History of the Koreans in Japan*, p. 167.

education issue exploded. The leaders of the Kobe branch of Chōren refused to vacate their schools by April 15, the appointed date. On the day before the deadline several thousand Koreans gathered in front of the prefectural governor's headquarters, and a committee demanded to speak with the governor. The governor refused to meet with them that day or the next, and the Japanese police finally dispersed the Koreans by force. On April 24 a crowd of 500 Koreans broke into the governor's private office and forced him to withdraw his order closing the Korean schools.

SCAP immediately proclaimed a state of emergency for the Kobe area, and several thousand Koreans were arrested. This was the only time during the entire occupation that a state of emergency had been declared.[42] The events in Kobe, in the spring of 1948 lost for the Koreans in Japan any sympathy that SCAP might have been willing to extend to their cause.

Suppression of Korean Communists

SCAP was now firmly convinced that Chōren and its affiliated organizations were not only communist dominated but a threat to SCAP's program of democratization for Japan. This decision was based on the Kobe violence and all activities of left-wing Koreans from the time the war ended to the spring of 1948.[43] For SCAP, the Koreans in Japan had

[42] Wagner, *The Korean Minority in Japan*, p. 72. Swearingen and Langer, *Red Flag in Japan*, p. 181.

[43] The Japanese Communist Party's policy toward the Koreans in Japan was clearly stated in *Zen-ei* (Vanguard), an official party publication: "The direction in which the six hundred thousand Koreans in Japan are moving, that is to say, whether or not they will constitute a strong wing in the struggle of Japan's revolutionary forces, is becoming of supreme importance. The significance of the issue is not so much a matter of sheer numbers but stems from the fact that these Koreans constitute an exploited, racial minority which had developed

become a security problem similar to the one that had plagued the prewar Japanese government, and SCAP acted in a similar manner by suppressing organizations it considered undesirable.

An official of Chōren denied that the Kobe riots had been communist inspired, but eight of the arrested Japanese communists claimed that the incident had been planned by party headquarters in Tokyo. Further investigation by the United States Army and the Japanese police supported the opinion that the incident had been organized by the Japanese Communist Party.[44]

The 350,000-member [45] Chōren gained an even stronger grip on the Korean community in Japan after the Kobe riots. The loss of the battle over education (Chōren temporarily retained control of 57 schools) gave Chōren "a heightened aura of martyrdom." After the formation of the Democratic Peoples Republic of Korea in 1948, Chōren became even more active and open in its communist activities. This led to the violation of many SCAP and Japanese directives and numerous fights with Japanese police.[46]

The conflict between SCAP and the Japanese government on the one hand and Chōren on the other hand reached a climax on September 8, 1949, when the Japanese government ordered the dissolution of Chōren and three other Korean left-wing groups. The four organizations were

an intense hatred for Japanese imperialism. . . . . their resistance and revolutionary fighting strength must be properly organized as part of Japan's democratic revolution. To consolidate the fighting power of these individuals and to guarantee that, ideologically and politically, they come under the influence of the Japanese Communist party is the fundamental task of Korean communists." Kim Tu-Yang, "The Korean Movement is Changing," *Zen-ei*, I (May 1, 1947), 38.

[44] Swearingen and Langer, *Red Flag in Japan*, p. 183.
[45] *Ibid.*
[46] Wagner, *The Korean Minority in Japan*, p. 84.

The Korean Minority in Occupied Japan

branded "anti-democratic and terroristic associations that resisted orders of the Allied Occupation."[47] Chōren refused to obey the government order and appealed to SCAP to reverse it. But the Japanese government eventually confiscated the assets of Chōren and closed the remaining schools under its jurisdiction.[48]

The mounting tension between Russia and the United States, the creation of communist China, and the outbreak of the Korean War caused SCAP increasingly to regard the Koreans in Japan as a security problem. The Japanese government acted promptly to meet the communist invasion of the Republic of Korea. Just two days after the invasion, on June 27, 1950, the government ordered *Akahata* (Red Flag), the official organ of the Japanese Communist Party, to cease publication.[49] By August 7, the left-wing Korean press also was suppressed. Premier Yoshida Shigeru stated that communist "fifth columnists" would be suppressed. The Japanese government acted to protect its internal security by reorganizing and doubling the size of the special investigation bureau of the attorney general's office and by creating a national police reserve of 70,000 men. Yoshida explained on the floor of the Diet that the national police reserve was solely "to protect public order against the dangers of communism."[50] The government also directed the police to keep close watch on the entire Korean population in Japan.[51]

---

[47] Swearingen and Langer, *Red Flag in Japan*, p. 183. This order did not apply to Mindan, the main rival of Chōren.

[48] The official career of Kim Ch'ŏn-hae, who had been the guiding power within Chōren, ended with the dissolution of the organization, but he continued to work in secret. A few days before the beginning of the Korean War he left Japan for North Korea, where he has remained as a highly placed official of the government.

[49] Swearingen and Langer, *Red Flag in Japan*, p. 243.

[50] *Ibid.*, pp. 251–252.

[51] Wagner, *The Korean Minority in Japan*, p. 91.

Despite the increased vigilance of SCAP and the Japanese government, the left-wing affiliated Koreans soon organized the Zainichi Chōsen Tōitsu Minshū Sensen, or Minsen (Koreans' United Democratic Front in Japan), with the aim of unifying the 600,000 Koreans in Japan in support of North Korea. Minsen, which had close contacts with the Japanese Communist Party, sabotaged the production and transportation of war materials destined for Korea, and raised funds for North Korea.[52]

During this period of increased tension and bitterness precipitated by the Korean conflict, the American occupation of Japan came to an end. The problems of the minority were even more complex than they had been seven years earlier, and the new Japanese government of Yoshida Shigeru was in no mood to brook interference by the Koreans, especially those with left-wing affiliations.

[52] *Current Phases* . . . , p. 61.

IX
THE KOREAN MINORITY IN "NEW JAPAN," 1952–1960

On September 8, 1951, Japan and 48 Allied Powers signed the peace treaty which ended six years of foreign occupation. The treaty did not go into effect, however, until April 28, 1952, after which Japan was free to exercise its own discretion in domestic and international affairs.

One of the first internal problems that engaged the attention of the new sovereign country was the status of the Korean minority. With SCAP's encouragement, Japan and the Republic of Korea began to debate the problem in October, 1951, before the treaty went into effect. The delegates of the two powers had many conferences but could not agree on the status of the minority. By October, 1953, the delegates had reached a deadlock, and negotiations were suspended. The status of the Koreans in Japan remained much as it had been during the occupation.[1]

[1] Heiji Shinozaki, *Zainichi Chōsenjin undō*, p. 23.

Korean Organizations

The Koreans in Japan, especially those active in the left-wing movement, were highly inflamed by the Korean War. Minsen had spread propaganda defending the actions of the North Koreans. It also collected money for the Democratic People's Republic of Korea and sent letters of encouragement to its troops. Mindan, in reply to the North Korean propaganda campaign, launched one of its own, condemning the aggression and "Red imperialism" of North Korea. Several hundred young Mindan supporters left for Korea and joined the South Korean army.[2]

As the war progressed, Minsen formed even closer ties with the Japanese Communist Party. Many Koreans became deeply involved in the party's attempt to seize power in Japan by fomenting internal revolution. Throughout 1951 and the first half of 1952, riots between communists and the Japanese police increased in industrial areas. Japanese communists and Korean supporters of Kim Il-sung usually formed the core of the disturbances. On May Day, 1952, large-scale riots erupted in Tokyo along with smaller ones in other parts of Japan. The huge Tokyo riot in the Imperial Palace Plaza resembled a battlefield and resulted in one death and more than a thousand casualties. Koreans played a conspicuous part in this bloody clash with the police in Tokyo and also in riots in other parts of Japan.[3]

After the Korean armistice in July, 1953, Minsen cooperated even more closely with the Japanese Communist Party.

---

[2] *Ibid.*, pp. 239–242. SCAP agreed to accept 750 volunteers. Only 725 actually went to Korea. Of these, 61 were killed. About 50 per cent returned to Japan and formed a veterans' association. Yu-gan Yi, *A Fifty-Year History of the Koreans in Japan*, pp. 138–139.

[3] Paul F. Langer and A. Rodger Swearingen, *Japanese Communism*, p. 79. Shinozaki, *Zainichi Chōsenjin undō*, pp. 220–221.

As a result, the Japanese government increased its security control over the Koreans in Japan. By 1954, however, Korean communists in both Japan and North Korea began to feel that Minsen's preoccupation with revolution in Japan was a mistake. The Korean communists were ordered by the northern regime to loosen their ties with the Japanese Communist Party and concentrate on Korean problems. The result was the dissolution of Minsen on May 26, 1955.[4]

Since the cessation of hostilities in Korea, the political configuration of Korean organizations in Japan has remained basically the same. Whether North Korean or South Korean sympathizers or neutral, each group had contacts with Japanese organizations that supported their activities, all closely connected with the politics of the Korean peninsula. Koreans in Japan were greatly affected by the fierce war that devastated their homeland. This costly and lengthy conflict so intensified the political differences of the Koreans in Japan that the pro-North and the pro-South groups were unable to agree on any issue.

The Zainichi Chōsenjin Sōrengōkai, or Chōsōren (General Federation of Korean Residents in Japan), organized in May, 1955, has since been the central organization in the pro-North group. Chōsōren, under the direct control of North Korea, was created to replace the dissolved Minsen. The new organization maintained its connection with the Japanese communist movement but, unlike the old Minsen, pursued a course designed to suit its own self-interest and did not allow itself to be used, as the older organization had done. Chōsōren had a twofold program: to protect the livelihood of Koreans in Japan and to promote the aims of North

[4] Public Security Investigation Agency, *Current Phases of the Activities of Korean Residents in Japan*, p. 3. Yi, *A Fifty-Year History of the Koreans in Japan*, p. 137.

Korea.[5] Ideally, the first half of the program should have engaged most of Chōsōren's attention and energy, but the organization has increasingly become an arm of North Korea's foreign office.

The organizational structure of Chōsōren followed the usual communist pattern in having all power held by the central headquarters. The headquarters in Tokyo comprised a central committee, an inspection committee, a central standing committee, and seven chairmen. Under this superstructure was the central secretariat, with seven main sections: secretariat, education, external affairs, social, economic, financial, and cultural and propaganda. The central headquarters directed the activities of four regional councils and forty-seven prefectural headquarters. Lower down the scale were 440 branches, 1,264 subbranches, and 1,265 circles. In 1957 Chōsōren had a membership of 89,868 under the nominal leadership of Han Duk-su. If the 64,915 members of affiliated organizations were included, the membership totaled 154,783.[6] Chōsōren announced as its goals: "(1) the peaceful unification of Korea, (2) the protection of Korean racial rights, (3) the promotion of racial education, [and] (4) the normalization of relations between North Korea and Japan."[7]

Under the supervision and with the financial support of North Korea, Chōsōren branched out in many directions with the aim of capturing leadership over all the 600,000 Koreans in Japan. Its propaganda network controlled the Chōsen Tsūshinsha (Korean News Agency), affiliated with the North Korean Central News Agency and the Pyongyang Broadcasting Station. For all practical purposes, the Chōsen

---

[5] *Current Phases* . . . , p. 3. Shakai undō chōsakai hen, *Sayoku dantai jiten*, p. 223.
[6] *Current Phases* . . . , pp. 3-4.
[7] *Ibid.*, pp. 7-13.

Tsūshinsha, which began to publish a daily newspaper, *Chōsen Tsūshin* (Korean News), became a branch of the North Korean Agency.[8] Chōsōren published other newspapers in Korean and Japanese and in 1960 began to publish a weekly in English. Through affiliated booksellers, Chōsōren became the importer and distributor of newspapers, magazines, and books published in North Korea. Significant imported books were translated into Japanese, English, and other languages. One company, the Gakushū Shobō, published Korean textbooks for Korean students in Japan.[9]

Chōsōren was concerned with the education of young Koreans in Japan and, three months after it was organized, created the Central Educational Institute, which worked closely with North Korea to oversee the direction of Korean education. Based on materials sent from North Korea, a new set of textbooks was designed for Korean children living in Japan. A Japanese Public Security Investigation Agency report, published in September, 1957, pointed out that Chōsōren was instructing Korean school children in Marxism and Leninism and was attempting to mold them into good communists.[10] Chōsōren also wanted to give Koreans an opportunity to receive a communist education at the university level by establishing the Chōsen Daigaku (Korean University) in April, 1956. The express purpose of this university was to provide new leadership that could be used by the northern regime.[11]

The pro-communist sympathy of Chōsōren was further exhibited in its effort to maintain connections with numerous other left-wing Korean groups in Japan, especially with

[8] *Sayoku dantai jiten*, p. 223.
[9] *Ibid.*, p. 224.
[10] *Current Phases* . . . , pp. 12–13.
[11] *Sayoku dantai jiten*, p. 230.

Zainichi Chōsenjin Shōrengōkai (Association of Korean Businessmen in Japan), Chōsen Chūō Geijutsu Dan (Korean Central Art Group), and Chōsen Mondai Kenkyūjo (Korea Problems Research Center). It also had close connections with sympathetic Japanese organizations, the most important of which were Nitchō Kyōkai (Japanese-Korean Society), Nitchō Bōeki Kai (Japanese-Korean Trade Society), and Zainichi Chōsenjin Kikoku Kyōryoku Kai (Cooperation Society for the Repatriation of Korean Nationals in Japan.[12]

Nitchō Kyōkai had been organized in June, 1951, by a group of Koreans and Japanese who sought to foster Korean culture and religion. At first they used the organization mainly to help Koreans suffering from the effects of the Korean War. By 1952, however, the communist element had captured the leadership of the organization, and Nitchō Kyōkai became active in left-wing politics. Most of the original members then left the organization, and by 1954 the association was little more than a name.[13]

In April, 1955, Hatanaka Masaharu attended the New Delhi Conference, a communist-sponsored four-day meeting of Asian and African states, and on his way home stopped in North Korea to confer with members of that government. In June he returned to Japan and became the new managing director of Nitchō Kyōkai.[14] Under his active leadership the organization quickly revived and, in November, 1955, held its first nationwide meeting. Its program was expressed in the slogan, "Let's have closer friendship and understanding between the Japanese and Korean peoples." Nitchō Kyōkai

[12] *Ibid.*, p. 224.
[13] *Ibid.*, pp. 235–236.
[14] Hatanaka Masaharu was formerly a Moscow-based reporter for the *Asahi Shinbun*. After the Second World War he left the newspaper to become a social and political critic. He is well known for his writings on the Soviet Union. *Ibid.*, p. 236.

took positive measures to bring the policy to fruition by advocating diplomatic relations and an economic and cultural exchange program between Japan and North Korea. It also declared itself in favor of the peaceful unification of Korea. Under Hatanaka's leadership the organization rapidly increased its membership and restored its close connection with Chōsōren.[15]

Mindan, which had been established in August, 1948, remained the central force in the pro-South grouping. Like Chōsōren, it had a central headquarters and several hundred branches. In 1957 its total membership, including affiliated groups, was 90,000.[16] Mindan, like Chōsōren, was dedicated to promoting the welfare of Koreans living in Japan. Mindan, also, was strongly anti-Japanese, especially during its early period. Unlike Chōsōren, however, it received little financial and moral support from Korea, at least until the fall of the Syngman Rhee government in April, 1960.

Plagued by factionalism and schisms, Mindan was often unable to present a united front in opposition to its arch rival, Chōsōren. While Chōsōren and North Korea worked in close cooperation to attain their goals in Japan, Mindan often feuded with its home government, especially in regard to the normalization of Japanese-Korean relations. During the late 1950's some members of Mindan exerted pressure on South Korea to speed up negotiations with the Japanese and to come to an agreement, in order to improve the position of the Koreans in Japan.

From its inception Mindan was the weaker of the two organizations. Its leadership, a relatively prosperous and conservative middle-class group, no longer fully identified with the majority of the Koreans. This leadership, lacking

[15] *Ibid.*, p. 237.
[16] *Current Phases* . . . , p. 20.

the ideological weapon so successfully employed by Chōsōren, found itself unable to capture the allegiance of the majority of the Koreans. The lack of a set goal, coupled with intense factionalism, doomed Mindan to a second position. Its inability to capture the leadership of the minority, after the government dissolved Chōren, robbed Mindan of perhaps its greatest chance to surpass its rival.

The most important problem, as Chōsōren so often declared, was the proper education of the Korean youth, and in this respect Mindan failed miserably. The Mindan youth league, for example, was led by men in their thirties and contained almost no members around twenty.[17] One Korean, a graduate from Tokyo University, explained the Chōsōren success this way: "The pro-North Koreans at Tokyo University were much more active. They held weekly discussions about Korean politics and they were more politically conscious."[18]

Because of Mindan's weakness, Chōsōren was in a better position to exploit the Korean minority and use it for its political purposes. The very manner in which the Koreans lived, with approximately 60 per cent clustered in Korean settlements, made the task much easier.[19] The fact that the Koreans in each community often came from the same area in Korea, spoke the same dialect, or were related by blood, made their manipulation easier. Those who refused to participate in Chōsōren's demonstrations and other activities were sometimes subjected to extreme pressure and might be completely ostracized.[20]

A third camp, between Chōsōren and Mindan, developed

---

[17] Yi, *A Fifty Year History of the Koreans in Japan*, p. 139.
[18] Personal interview, Tokyo, August 3, 1961.
[19] *Asahi Shinbun*, March 29, 1965, p. 12.
[20] In Ha Lee and Jean E. Sonnenfeld, "Koreans in Japan: Conflict or Reconciliation?," *The Japan Christian Quarterly*, XXV (October, 1959), 301.

during the 1950's. but this group remained small. The author and journalist Kim Sam-kyu established the Chōsen Chūritsuka Undō Iinkai (Korean Committee for the Neutralization of Korea), or KCNK, in 1957. This committee, with Kim as its president, presented a plan to unite the peninsula under one government. Both governments, the South and the North, were to be liquidated and replaced by a single unified state by agreement among the great powers. The latter were to guarantee that free elections be held throughout the peninsula. Next, the Korean people would choose deputies to draft a constitution for a united Korea. The new state would be truly neutral in world affairs, supporting neither side in the cold war. Kim's group propagated its plan through the *Koria Hyōron* (Korea Review), published from September, 1957, to August, 1961.[21] The KCNK was criticized by both Chōsōren and Mindan, neither of which was connected with a government willing to give up its sovereignty for the sake of Korean unity. This third group among Koreans in Japan received much publicity but gained little power.

Three Major Sources of Disputes

In January, 1948, the government informed the Koreans that they must abide by the laws regulating Japanese schools. They were to use the Japanese language and Japanese textbooks in classes. Korean schools must be registered with local authorities, and the teachers were required to have teaching certificates. The Japanese Education Ministry was particularly anxious to put a stop to the communist education being given to Korean students in schools conducted by Chōren. Most of the Koreans, however, refused

[21] Kim's plan for unification is presented in *Chōsen no shinjitsu*, pp. 159–160. The *Korea Review* resumed publication in May, 1964.

to obey the directives of the Education Ministry. Chōren and schools under its control was dissolved by government decree in September, 1949.[22] The following month, all Korean schools throughout Japan were ordered to disband or reorganize, and their students to enroll in Japanese schools.[23]

Koreans often refer to the time between 1949 and the spring of 1955 as the "dark period" (kurai jidai) for Korean education in Japan. More and more Korean schools were being closed, and those that remained open temporarily were not allowed to teach in Korean or to display pictures of Kim Il-sung.[24] It was during this period, on April 28, 1952, that the peace treaty came into effect and the Koreans in Japan officially became foreigners. Under their new status they were no longer eligible to operate public schools and could maintain only private institutions.[25] The Korean schools which complied with Education Ministry standards for construction, certification of teachers, and courses were allowed to continue or to reopen. More important, the Koreans were allowed much latitude in the private school curriculum, which had been denied to them earlier. The new private Korean schools were permitted to teach in Korean provided they taught Japanese as a second language.

The primary emphasis in all Korean schools in Japan had been teaching of the Korean language, for Korean children were growing up unable to speak their "native" tongue. After 1955, Chōsōren-affiliated schools kept records of how well new first-graders understood Korean: 40 per cent of them could not write their own name in Korean, 77

[22] Shinozaki, *Zainichi Chōsenjin undō*, p. 22.
[23] *Ibid.* Edward W. Wagner, *The Korean Minority in Japan*, p. 85.
[24] Rōdōsha ruporutāju shūdan, *Nihonjin no mita zainichi Chōsenjin*, p. 71.
[25] Shinozaki, *Zainichi Chōsenjin undō*, p. 170.

per cent could not say their parents' names in Korean, and only 8 per cent were able to say simple words like "pencil" and "desk" in their mother tongue.[26]

The Korean schools taught their pupils to take pride in their ethnic background. The language, history, and geography of Korea formed the backbone of the curriculum.[27] Chōsōren schools modeled their educational program upon that of North Korea and began to indoctrinate their students with the same communist educational material used in the northern part of the peninsula.[28] The primary purpose was the creation of a younger generation of "enthusiastic patriots" devoted to the "fatherland." Students were indoctrinated with anti-Japanese sentiments.[29] At the Chōsōren schools, all classes, except for two hours of Japanese a week, were taught in Korean.[30]

After 1955 the schools affiliated with the northern regime continued to be more numerous than those of the rival Mindan group. This situation can be attributed mainly to South Korea's failure to send financial aid to Mindan. North Korea, in contrast, made the education of the Korean youth in Japan a special concern, and by 1960 it had sent twelve times as much money as South Korea.[31] The aggressive policy of North Korea resulted, by 1960, in the creation of 280 schools under its control compared with only 50 for South Korea.[32]

A second dispute which has plagued relations between the Japanese and the Koreans in Japan since 1952 arose over

[26] *Nihonjin no mita zainichi Chōsenjin*, p. 77.
[27] *Ibid.*, pp. 69–70.
[28] *Current Phases* . . . , p. 13.
[29] *The People's Korea*, January 15, 1961, p. 4.
[30] *Nihonjin no mita zainichi Chōsenjin*, pp. 74–75.
[31] North Korea sent 1,200,000,000 yen compared to South Korea's 100,000,000. *The Korean Republic*, April 15, 1961, p. 2.
[32] *Ibid.*

government grants to unemployed Koreans. In May, 1950, the government promulgated the Livelihood Protection Law, which was applied to Korean residents in Japan after the peace treaty came into effect in April, 1952.[33] Many Koreans in Japan lived close to the edge of poverty, and any adverse shift in the economy caused unemployment and destitution among them. Therefore, many of them received funds from the government under the livelihood protection law. Between 1952 and 1956 Koreans received about 2,600,000,000 yen annually; the number of recipients was ten times higher for Koreans than for Japanese.[34]

In 1955 the Welfare Ministry, after a nationwide investigation, advocated a drastic reduction in payments, but Koreans and Japanese protested, and only moderate cuts were made.[35] From 1956 to 1963 individual payments were increased and the Koreans annually received an average of about 2,800,000,000 yen in support payments.[36]

The third controversial issue was registration. Between 1947 and 1959, Korean residents were ordered to undergo registration three times. Chōsōren, objecting especially to fingerprinting, led the fight against the government-ordered registration. In cooperation with Japanese left-wing groups, Chōsōren attempted to bring the dispute to the floor of the Diet and turn it into a major political battle. Each time, however, the government safely skirted the issue and enforced the registration.[37]

[33] "Koreans in Japan (2)," *Korea Journal*, II (May, 1962).
[34] *Current Phases* . . . , p. 9.
[35] *Ibid.*, p. 10.
[36] In 1955 the number of Koreans receiving payments was 120,000, but by 1963 this figure had dropped to 59,000. The Welfare Ministry, after temporarily cutting payments in 1955, gradually increased individual monthly payments from 1,964 yen in 1955 to 4,770 yen in 1963. Personal interview with Matsuda Yasuhiko, October 23, 1964, in Tokyo.
[37] *Current Phases* . . . , p. 12.

General Condition of the Minority

By February, 1960, the Korean minority amounted to 613,671; this was nine-tenths of the total number of foreigners living in Japan. Among this number, 444,586 had chosen to register as citizens of North Korea and 162,871 as citizens of South Korea.[38] Every prefecture and municipal area in Japan had some Korean residents, but the largest numbers were concentrated in the Osaka and Tokyo areas.

As in the past, the Koreans continued to live near each other; their dwellings were usually clustered together in what were called "Korean villages." [39] The economic life of Korean residents was little changed from that of the prewar period; many were unemployed. Of the employed, the majority were unskilled laborers. Others ran dance halls, pachinko (a type of pinball) parlors, motion picture theaters, and restaurants. A few managed to enter the upper ranks of Japanese business and intellectual life, but, for the most part, Koreans were excluded from the main stream of Japanese economic life. As a result, they led a precarious existence and were very vulnerable in periods of economic depression. In June, 1959, 14 per cent of Koreans received financial support from the Japanese government. Because of their marginal existence, Koreans often turned to illegal activities such as illicit manufacture of liquor and traffic in narcotics. This helps to explain why the Korean criminal rate was six times that of the Japanese.[40]

---

[38] Kaigai jijo chosa hen, *Chōsen Yōran*, p. 173. In September, 1963, there were 571,676 Koreans registered with the Ministry of Justice; thus 88 per cent of the foreigners living in Japan were Korean. Not included in these figures were 25,723 Koreans who had become Japanese citizens (from April 28, 1952, to the end of 1962). Hōmushō nyūkoku kanrikyoku hen, *Shutsunyūkoku kanri to sono jittai*, pp. 85–86, 91–92.

[39] *Chōsen yōran*, p. 173.

[40] *Ibid. Current Phases* . . . , p. 29. Several years earlier the percentage of Koreans receiving financial aid from the Japanese govern-

The Japanese attitude is revealed in several public opinion polls taken between 1954 and 1959. In the fall of 1954, 246 university students and 168 adults of Kumamoto city, Kyushu, were asked to register their feelings about 18 "races." They were particularly hostile toward the Koreans, who were rated as the most disliked people. The report compiled from this data pointed out that although there has always been conflict between the two "races," this conflict became especially sharp after the end of the Second World War. The increase in mutual antagonism was attributed to the sudden change in status of both groups which came with the defeat of Japan.[41] Another poll was taken in 1959, with university students in Kumamoto as subjects. The results were exactly the same in regard to Koreans; again they were rated as the most disliked "race."[42] Similar surveys made in Osaka and Tokyo gave the same results. In 1959, when 393 students of all levels in Osaka were offered

ment was considerably higher: in December, 1955, the figure was over 24 per cent. One Japanese scholar estimated that in some prefectures, during the same year, about half of the Koreans received government-financed aid. Yi, *A Fifty-Year History of the Korean Minority in Japan*, pp. 155–157. A Korean writer estimates that at present about 30 per cent of the prostitutes in Tokyo and Osaka are Koreans. Jun Den, "Rokujūmannin no minashigo, Amerika ni okeru kokujin no sonzai ni mo hisubeki rokujūman no zainichi Chōsenjin mondai ni me o tojite wa naranu," *Bungei Shunjū*, XLI (October, 1963), 145. It was extremely difficult for Koreans to obtain a job with a Japanese company even if they had degrees from a Japanese university. Many Korean university graduates were forced to work as truck drivers, day laborers, or ragpickers. Even though Koreans had to pay taxes, they could not become beneficiaries of the national health insurance plan, had difficulty in getting bank loans, and were not eligible to live in the Public Housing Corporation apartments. Kyoko Baba, "The Sad Lot of Japan's Korean Residents," *The Japan Times*, June 18, 1964, p. 5.

[41] Takamasa Kuzutani, "Shominzoku ni taisuru kōaku taido no kenkyū," *Kyōiku Shinrigaku Kenkyū*, III (July, 1955), 39–57.

[42] Kuzutani, "Minzokuteki kōaku to sono jinkakuteki akuin," *ibid.*, VIII (June, 1960), 8–17.

11 "racial" groups to rank, they also listed Koreans at the bottom.[43]

In September, 1951, Izumi Seiichi, a professor of anthropology at Tokyo University, interviewed 344 Japanese of the lower middle class in Tokyo to ascertain their feelings about other "races." In this survey the Koreans ranked next to last, with the Negro taking the lowest position. When those interviewed were asked which "race" they actively disliked, Koreans were named with greatest frequency (150 times). Izumi inquired into the reasons for this hostility, and found that the Koreans were considered dirty, "blackhearted" (haraguroi), cunning, and of a lower cultural level. The Japanese also believed that the Koreans held Japan in contempt and would harm the nation both economically and politically if given the opportunity. Izumi concluded that Japanese feelings toward Koreans were not based on any notion that they were "qualitatively abnormal, but on a well-established 'stereotype of hatred.' "[44]

The Diplomacy of Korean Repatriation

The two Koreas present a complicated diplomatic dilemma for Japan.[45] Former colonies and mother countries often engage in bitter exchanges after the old ties have been broken, but in the end some compromise is usually reached. For Japan and the two Koreas no solution had been reached by 1960, and the three countries maintained no formal diplomatic relations. The issues in this diplomatic triangle grew more complicated with each year. The military divi-

[43] Tatsuo Haratani, "Minzokuteki sutereotaipu to kōaku kanjō ni tsuite no kōsatsu," *ibid.*, VIII (June, 1960), 1–7.
[44] Ivan I. Morris, *Nationalism and the Right Wing in Japan*, p. 70.
[45] William J. Jorden, "Japan's Diplomacy between East and West," in *Japan between East and West*, p. 250.

sion of Korea in 1945, the formation of Red China, the Korean War, and the cold war between the communist and noncommunist powers made the establishment of normal relations between Japan and the two Koreas almost impossible.

The status of the Korean minority in Japan was a point of dispute between that country and the two Koreas. Both the South and the North insist that it alone represents the true legal government of Korea, and each declares itself the only spokesman for the Korean minority in Japan. Both countries have used the minority as a lever in their negotiations with the Japanese, and for both it is a matter of international prestige to capture the allegiance of the Koreans in Japan. Japan had no formal diplomatic relations with South Korea, but she did recognize it as the legitimate government of Korea. Consequently, South Korean legal ties with the minority in Japan were always much closer than those of the North Korean government. Both Japan and South Korea were administered by American military governments, so the two countries were often forced by the United States to cooperate. Under the aegis of SCAP, Seoul established a quasi-diplomatic mission in Japan, and in 1951 bilateral negotiations at Tokyo were initiated with the support of the United States.

Korea was not a formal participant in either the Second World War or the peace conference of September, 1951, in San Francisco. Therefore it was necessary for Korea and Japan to reach a private agreement upon the many issues between them. In preliminary discussions held in Tokyo during October and November, 1951, participants agreed to discuss the legal status of Koreans in Japan, the question of ownership of Japanese vessels in Korean waters at the end of the war, Japanese claims to compensation for properties formerly held in Korea, fishery questions, and diplomatic relations.[46] South Korea and Japan, by their consideration of these matters, seemed to be taking appropriate measures toward settling their outstanding differences.

A committee was created to discuss the problem of the Korean minority in Japan, particularly nationality, permanent residence, and legal status. South Korea insisted that the Koreans be given a special status, receiving all the benefits of full Japanese citizenship but remaining citizens of South Korea.[47] The preliminary discussions seemed to be making progress, but it soon became evident that negotiations would be a long and painful process for both sides.

Syngman Rhee, president of the Republic of Korea, developed an intense hatred for the Japanese during his many years of exile. He never ceased vilifying the Japanese and seemed to take delight in irritating them. The Japanese government also had its share of officials who could not forget Korea's former status under Japan, and who enjoyed reminding Koreans of the past. Under such conditions the negotiations between the two countries were almost doomed to failure. In January, 1952, President Rhee established the "Peace Line" (called the "Rhee Line" by the Japanese), which extended into the Sea of Japan about 60 miles from the Korean coast. The government declared the area inside this line territorial waters of South Korea and began to arrest all Japanese fishermen caught within its boundaries.[48] The Japanese denounced Rhee's action. The two governments were also engaged in a territorial dispute over some islands, the small and rocky Takeshima group (Bamboo Islands, or "Tokto" in Korean). The Koreans settled the

[46] R. Allan Dionisopoulos, "Japanese-Korean Relations," *Midwest Journal of Political Science*, I (May, 1957), 61.

[47] "Koreans in Japan (2)," *Korea Journal*, II (May, 1962), 19. Douglas Mendel, *The Japanese People and Foreign Policy*, p. 177.

[48] *Ibid.*, pp. 173–174.

dispute in their favor by sending an armed force to occupy the islands in 1953.[49] As a result, negotiations between South Korea and Japan were suspended in October, 1953, with none of the problems solved.

The government under President Rhee sometimes spoke of the rights of the Korean minority in Japan, especially when negotiating with the Japanese, but it offered little concrete aid to the Koreans in Japan.[50] Rhee's government could have worked through Mindan to gain the leadership of the minority, but chose not to do so. South Korea might have financed the building of Mindan's school system and sent officials to oversee the work, but for the most part this policy was not followed. President Rhee was content to use the Koreans in Japan as a lever in diplomatic dealings with the Japanese. Later his government paid heavily for this error.

In contrast to the policy followed by President Rhee, the People's Republic, especially after the Korean War, began to display great interest in the affairs of the minority. By 1955, the northern regime had attained a position of strength from which to speak for the Koreans in Japan. In that year, when the Koreans in Japan registered with the Japanese government, more than 75 per cent signed as citizens of North Korea,[51] and the Japanese government could

[49] *Ibid.*, p. 176. These islands are in the Sea of Japan about midway between Japan and Korea.

[50] Tatsuo Mitarai, "Korea-Japan Diplomacy," *The Oriental Economist*, XXVI (April, 1958), 190. Mindan, after a decade of waiting for aid from Seoul, publicly criticized the South Korean attitude on June 15, 1959. The association "issued a dramatic resolution declaring that it 'could no longer trust or support South Korea.' It said bitterly that 'the Seoul government had completely abandoned them in their struggle' and revealed that 'for the past ten years it had been requesting funds from Seoul without success.' " Kiwon Chung, "Japanese-North Korean Relations Today," *Asian Survey*, IV (April, 1964), 800.

[51] *Nihon kindaishi jiten*, p. 217.

no longer ignore it when discussing the minority. North Korea had much to gain by courting the minority. The Koreans in Japan could supplement her manpower shortage, they could be used as a tool in her diplomatic negotiations with the Japanese, and their allegiance would be a diplomatic triumph over South Korea and the United States.

Between 1953 and 1957 South Korea and Japan occasionally held informal talks, but none of these meetings were fruitful. The government of South Korea insisted that compensation be paid to the Koreans in Japan before they were repatriated; the Japanese demanded that fishermen seized by the Korean navy be returned. When the Japanese government announced its intention to send some Koreans to the Democratic People's Republic, South Korea protested vehemently. President Rhee was especially adamant in his attitude toward Japan. Repeatedly he told the press that the Japanese still planned to conquer Korea and were only waiting until they were strong enough.[52] South Korea, however, continued to pay little attention to the Korean minority in Japan until after Rhee's removal.

The Democratic People's Republic of Korea, in contrast, never missed an opportunity to stress its deep and legitimate concern for the fate of the Koreans in Japan. In August, 1954, Foreign Minister Nam Il stated that it was the "consistent policy" of his government to protect the rights of Koreans in Japan,[53] and in December, 1955, he repeated

[52] *The Korean Information Bulletin,* November-December, 1957.
[53] Democratic People's Republic of Korea, *On the Question of the 600,000 Koreans in Japan,* p. 22. On August 30, for the first time since the establishment of the People's Republic, Nam Il charged the Japanese government with "suppressing the democratic rights of the Korean citizens living in Japan." Chung, "Japanese-North Korean Relations Today," p. 791. Since 1954 the North Korean government has repeatedly accused the Japanese government of persecuting the Ko-

this message.[54] Premier Kim Il-sung, in his April, 1956, report to the central committee of the Worker's party, invited Korean students in Japan to come to North Korea to be educated at the expense of the state.[55] The Northern government also announced its "sacred duty" to defend the rights of the Koreans in Japan, and demanded for them a stabilized life, the legitimate rights due foreigners, release of Koreans interned in camps, a guarantee of their return home, and freedom to run their own educational program in Japan.[56]

In August, 1958, at the celebration of the tenth anniversary of the founding of the People's Republic, Kim Il-sung offered the Koreans in Japan a new life in North Korea, and promised them "all conditions for leading a new life after their return to the homeland."[57] The Koreans in Japan were very enthusiastic about this offer. A contributor to the *Chūō Kōron* (Central Review), a Japanese monthly, wrote in December, 1958, "In many parts of the country I met many old [Korean] men who told me that this is the greatest joy they ever had."[58]

The northern regime showed its real interest in the Koreans of Japan by sending 1,200,000,000 yen to Japan between 1945 and 1960 for educational purposes. During this same period South Korea sent only 100,000,000 yen.[59] North

reans in Japan. The latest charge was made on July 11, 1964, by Radio Pyongyang. *The Japan Times*, July 13, 1964, p. 3.
[54] *On the Question* . . . , p. 26.
[55] Democratic People's Republic of Korea, *Third Congress of the Workers' Party of Korea*, p. 74.
[56] *On the Question* . . . , p. 33.
[57] Il-sung Kim, "Report at the Celebration Meeting of the Tenth Anniversary of the Founding of the Democratic People's Republic of Korea," *New Korea*, No. 29 (October, 1958), 20.
[58] Unai Fujishima *et al.*, "Zainichi Chōsenjin rokujūmannin no genjitsu," *Chūō Kōron*, LXXIII (December, 1958), 191.
[59] *The Korean Republic*, April 15, 1961, p. 2.

Korea, working closely with Chōsōren, presented a united front to the Japanese government.

One of the prime objectives of the diplomacy of North Korea was to prevent the successful conclusion of negotiations between Japan and the Republic of Korea. Rhee's unbending attitude helped the northern regime in its drive to attain that goal. The developments that led to the repatriation of Koreans from Japan to North Korea illustrate how the northern diplomats, with the aid of Chōsōren and other groups in Japan, gained a diplomatic victory over their compatriots to the south of the thirty-eighth parallel.

The South Korean delegates demanded that Japan pay compensation to the Koreans who were in Japan during the war, and refused to consider repatriation until this problem, and all other problems being negotiated, was settled. The North Koreans skillfully attacked the position of South Korea by offering to repatriate all the Koreans in Japan and to pay the entire cost of the operation. Besides, they waived any claims to compensation for the Koreans, since the repatriation of the Koreans in Japan was a "purely humanitarian" issue. They accused the Japanese and the Republic of Korea of attempting to make political capital out of the problem.[60] Chōsōren and Nitchō Kyōkai backed North Korea's stand with propaganda blasts and demonstrations in Japan. In May, 1959, the two organizations held a joint nationwide meeting on this subject in Tokyo and demanded that the government of Japan accept North Korea's plan for repatriation.[61]

Through Chōsōren and other sympathetic organizations in Japan, the northern government stepped up its propaganda barrage, urging the Koreans in Japan to return to

[60] *On the Question* . . . , pp. 128–129.
[61] *Sayoku dantai jiten*, p. 236.

the fatherland and take part in the building of a new state and a better life. The hard lot of the Koreans in Japan and the economic failure of South Korea were emphasized. The Koreans were told of the great "leaps forward" made by North Korea, and were given a glowing account of life in the northern half of the peninsula. The obvious economic progress of North Korea, in contrast to the economic decay and political corruption in South Korea, gave the propaganda added impact. Through the Japanese language publications under its control in Japan, the northern regime attacked the "Japanese imperialists" who, in conjunction with the United States, were said to prevent the normalization of North Korean diplomatic relations with Japan. In short, the northern government played on the theme that the Japanese masses were true friends who desired closer contacts with North Korea, and that only the reactionary policies of the Japanese leaders were preventing rapprochement.[62] Japanese politicians, journalists, and business leaders unofficially visited North Korea and signed joint declarations with North Korean representatives demanding the normalization of diplomatic relations between the two countries. The majority of these Japanese were supporters or leaders of various left-wing movements in Japan. The leader of Nitchō Kyōkai, Hatanaka Masaharu, again visited North Korea in June, 1960.[63]

The Democratic People's Republic of Korea prepared the stage well for Kim Il-sung's announcement of August, 1958, that all Koreans were welcome to return to North Korea from Japan. Two years earlier, in June, 1956, the premier had issued Cabinet Order 53, declaring that repatriated Koreans were to be given jobs, personal expense

---

[62] *On the Question* . . . , p. 38.
[63] *Ibid.*, p. 26. *Sayoku dantai jiten*, pp. 236–237.

money, loans to establish businesses, and medicines, clothing, and blankets. Their children were to be sent to school and given "preferential treatment," and the repatriates were to be lodged in "preferred homes." Each adult was to receive 20,000 won and each child under fifteen 10,000 won.[64] Such generous terms were bound to appeal to the Korean residents, and North Korea's willingness to drop the compensation issue and its pledge to pay for the entire repatriation appealed to the Japanese government.

The Republic of Korea replied to the diplomatic move of the northern regime by reminding the Japanese that only the southern government had the legal right to speak for the Koreans in Japan and that none of them could be repatriated without its permission. On March 11, 1957, Foreign Minister Cho Chung-whan sent a strongly worded statement to the Japanese government warning it against sending Koreans to Communist North Korea. Such a repatriation would be considered "an unfriendly act." His country could not "enter into normal and friendly relations with any government that would commit such a crime against the cause of freedom and democracy."[65]

Self-interest soon outweighed any moral obligations Japan might have held for the Korean Republic. The government of Kishi Nobusuke decided in 1958 to negotiate with North Korea on the repatriation of the Koreans in Japan, and, on February 13, 1959, gave its consent. The details were discussed by representatives of the Japanese and the North Korean Red Cross societies in Geneva between April and June. The International Red Cross agreed to aid the two national societies only after they had agreed on the

[64] *On the Question* . . . , p. 18.
[65] *Speeches and Statements by Foreign Minister Chung W. Cho*, pp. 84–85.

basic details. By June 24 the two national Red Cross societies reached an agreement which was later formally ratified in Calcutta on August 13, 1959. The International Red Cross was to supervise the repatriation by sending a committee to Japan.[66]

The Repatriation

The Calcutta Agreement provided that any Korean residing in Japan was free to apply for repatriation to North Korea. Application was to be made through the Japanese Red Cross, which would register persons who wished to be repatriated. The international committee of the Red Cross was to supervise the registration to ensure that the procedure "be fair, impartial, and in conformity with humanitarian principles." The Japanese Red Cross agreed to pay the cost of transporting and caring for the repatriates up to the point of embarkation, after which they were to become the responsibility of the North Korean government.[67] On August 13, 1959, the director of the public information bureau of the Japanese Foreign Ministry issued a statement that repatriation was being carried out on the "basis of the principle of the freedom of choice of residence." The Ko-

[66] International Committee of the Red Cross, "The International Committee and the Repatriation of Koreans Resident in Japan," *Revue Internationale de la Croix-Rouge*, Supplement, XIII (April, 1960), 63–68. Under the leadership of Chōsōren the left-wing forces in Japan launched a drive to force the Kishi government to accept the repatriation proposals of North Korea. "The response in Japan . . . was widespread. All political parties from the LDP to the JCP united to support the repatriation issue on a bipartisan basis. Almost all prefecture assemblies adopted unanimously a resolution in favor of repatriation." Chung, "Japanese-North Korean Relations Today," p. 797.
[67] Consulate General of Japan, "Korean Repatriation Agreement Signed," *Japan Report*, V (September, 1959), 3–4.

The Korean Minority in "New Japan"

reans were free to remain in Japan or to leave for either South or North Korea.[68] The Kishi government thus made it clear that its decision was based on humanitarian grounds.

The Rhee government in South Korea viewed the repatriation plan as a "monstrous scheme" to send the Koreans into slavery, and threatened to stop the repatriation ships by force. Rhee also offered to accept all those taken forcibly to Japan.[69] His offer, however, came too late. South Korea had attempted to utilize the Korean minority as pawns in the game of diplomatic chess, only to find that the Japanese had tired of the game.

In the spring of 1959 the North Korean government prepared for the return of the repatriates. A reception committee of high-placed government officials, led by First Vice-Premier Kim Il, was created to supervise the repatriation, with the Korean Red Cross taking care of details.[70] The Japanese Red Cross established an embarkation center just outside the seaport of Niigata on the Japan Sea side of Honshu. Nitchō Kyōkai also established a branch office in Niigata and worked closely with the two Red Cross societies.[71] On December 14, 1959, the first shipload of 975 sailed for North Korea on a Soviet vessel.[72] By December 11, 1960, the

[68] *Ibid.*, p. 3. According to some reports, Chōsōren applied force to make certain the repatriation was a success. In December, 1959, Korean communists daily visited the homes in one Korean village near Tokyo "in an effort to intimidate the residents into going to North Korea." Dan Kurzman, *Kishi and Japan*, pp. 365–366.

[69] *The New York Times*, March 2, 1959, p. 19; Aug. 14, 1959, p. 5. Foreign Minister Cho added specific "conditions" to Rhee's offer: the Japanese must "pay compensation for the forced labor previously imposed upon the residents" and the Koreans be allowed to take "all their property with them." Chung, "Japanese-North Korean Relations Today," p. 800.

[70] *On the Question* . . . , p. 19.

[71] *Sayoku dantai jiten*, p. 236.

[72] *The New York Times*, December 14, 1959, p. 14.

number of Koreans repatriated to North Korea had reached 51,325.[73]

It is impossible to determine how much the Kishi government was motivated by humanitarian reasons and how much by self-interest. The repatriation of substantial numbers of Koreans was bound to lessen the pressure of the minority in Japan. Each shipload represented that many more Koreans who could never again apply for subsidy under the provisions of the Livelihood Protection Law or march through the streets of Tokyo linked arm in arm with Japanese communists calling for the destruction of the government. The repatriation of the Koreans to North Korea provided a partial solution to one of the most pressing problems of Japan.

[73] *Ibid.,* December 12, 1960, p. 9. The repatriation of the Koreans to North Korea, since it constituted the first large-scale movement from a democratic society to a communist nation, caused much speculation about its motivation. The basic reason for this "reverse-course" migration seems to have been economic. The Japanese Red Cross issued a statement on June 26, 1959, that 75 per cent of the Koreans who were registered to return to North Korea were unemployed. In North Korea, in contrast to their situation in Japan, Koreans were offered employment, education, and decent living conditions. W. D. Reeve, *The Republic of Korea,* p. 59. See also *The Japan Times,* June 18, 1964, p. 5. Although the majority of the repatriates had originally come from South Korea (excluding those born in Japan), the confused economic and political situation in that country made it unattractive as a future home. Also, Japanese prejudice against the Koreans probably entered into the decision.

X
THE UNIFICATION ISSUE: THE INTENSIFICATION OF POLITICAL ACTIVITY, 1960–1963

Political activities of the Korean organizations in Japan intensified between 1960 and 1963. This new flurry was precipitated by Chōsōren in the late autumn of 1960, when that group, acting under orders from Pyongyang, began a movement for the unification of Korea. At the same time, Chōsōren launched a renewed opposition to the negotiations between Japan and South Korea, which it claimed were designed to reintroduce Japanese imperialism into the peninsula. The supporters of the northern regime maintained that the settlement of the long-standing diplomatic impasse between Japan and South Korea would dash all hope of unification. Chōsōren and its supporting Japanese organizations also initiated a determined propaganda drive against the United States, which they blamed for most of the ills that plagued Korea.

The confused political and economic situation in South

Korea helped to promote unrest among the politically active Koreans in Japan. After the fall of President Syngman Rhee in 1960, the Mindan organization seemed near collapse, but the coup of May 16, 1961, and the emergence of the highly nationalistic government of General Park Chung-hee infused new vigor into that group. Park's government countered the Chōsōren propaganda campaign by giving Mindan increased financial aid and moral support.

The Fall of the Rhee Government

Early in 1960 the Republic of Korea announced that an election for president and vice-president would be held on March 15. The Liberal Party of President Rhee was anxious to win this particular election, especially the vice-presidential office. Syngman Rhee was in his eighty-fifth year, and it was doubtful that he would live through another term in office. The Liberal Party stuffed ballot boxes and resorted to other fraudulent practices, with the result that their vice-presidential candidate won.[1] Within a few days students began to protest against the fraudulent elections and to demand new ones. Day by day the demonstrations grew larger and more insistent. The Liberal Party attempted to stop the students by force. On April 19, 1960, the government issued orders to fire on the students, and 115 were killed. President Rhee resigned, and the prospective vice-president and his family committed suicide. During the year that followed Rhee's resignation the Republic was plagued with one political crisis after another.

The Unification Issue

As economic and political conditions deteriorated in South Korea, the communist regime to the north was quick to

[1] Richard C. Allen, *Korea's Syngman Rhee*, pp. 226–227.

take advantage of the confused situation. On November 19, 1960, the Supreme People's Assembly made detailed plans for the unification of the country, advocating general elections and the withdrawal of all United States forces. The northern government also proposed the resumption of intercourse between the two countries and the reconstruction of the southern economy.[2] Chōsōren and its affiliated organizations held mass meetings in Tokyo, Osaka, and other Japanese cities to promote North Korea's unification plan.[3] Openly admitting that it conformed "firmly to the foreign policy of the Government of the Democratic People's Republic of Korea," Chōsōren prepared for a massive campaign to unify the Koreans in Japan behind the proposal.[4] It also wanted to win the Japanese people over to its cause. The left-wing Koreans in Japan were now involved in the international struggles of the cold war.

The United States was branded by the northern regime as the "most rabid enemy of the Asian peoples" and was accused of remilitarizing the "Japanese imperialists" for use as shock troops in an attempt to reconquer Korea. To unify Korea, the North Korean government and its organs in Japan demanded the withdrawal of the Americans and the Japanese from Korea.[5]

The northern regime and its agent in Japan, Chōsōren, still basking in the warmth of their stunning repatriation victory, waxed stronger as the southern government grew weaker. As a result, many Koreans who had sided with the Republic of Korea became discouraged and succumbed to Chōsōren's propaganda. Chōsōren sensed this attitude of defeatism and offered to meet with Mindan groups to discuss

[2] *The People's Korea*, January 1, 1961, p. 1.
[3] *Ibid.*, p. 2.
[4] *Ibid.*, p. 1.
[5] General Association of Korean Residents in Japan, *For Further Promoting Peaceful Unification of Korea*, pp. 14–15.

the issues of unification and of the Koreans in Japan. In January, 1961, journalists from both ideological camps met to discuss ways of unifying Korea. Chōsōren continued to hold meetings throughout Japan, promoting the unification plan.[6]

Japanese supporters of Chōsōren also staged demonstrations demanding discontinuation of the talks between Japan and South Korea and advocating the unification plan proposed by the northern regime. Socialist and communist members of the Diet denounced the United States-Japan security treaty and the negotiations between Japan and South Korea. While interpellating Prime Minister Ikeda Hayato, these Diet members charged that the negotiations were designed to obstruct the peaceful unification of Korea. They also demanded that North Korea be included in any talks that concerned the entire Korean people.[7]

Chōsōren's propaganda campaign reaped impressive results on March 1 when more than sixty Korean intellectuals, supporters of both North and South Korea, met at a restaurant in Tokyo and adopted a resolution to stage a combined cultural program. One Mindan supporter explained that he supported the policies of the South Korean government, but that it was "impossible to resist the current of the times."[8]

Throughout the rest of March, April, and May, the unification program gathered momentum in Japan. Nitchō Kyōkai and the Japanese Communist Party participated in mixed rallies with Chōsōren groups throughout the country. A Chōsōren rally held in Tokyo on March 27 was addressed by Hatanaka Masaharu, the head of Nitchō Kyōkai, and Ii Yashiro, a representative of the Japanese Communist Party.

[6] *The People's Korea*, February 1, 1961, p. 3.
[7] *Ibid.*, February 10, 1961, p. 3.
[8] *The Japan Times*, March 2, 1961, p. 1.

Han Duk-su, the leader of Chōsōren, was chairman of the meeting.[9] Left-wing Japanese also held independent meetings advocating unification. On April 19 more than 6,000 Japanese rallied to hear Kanemitsu Hososako of the Japanese Socialist Party, and Nozaka Sanzō, chairman of the Japanese Communist Party, express their support for the activities of Chōsōren and North Korea.[10]

During the spring of 1961 a unification drive, spearheaded by students in Seoul, was gaining momentum in South Korea. On April 19, the first anniversary of the fall of Rhee, 100,000 students and citizens of Seoul held a rally and demonstration. Many carried placards with such slogans as "No Life without Unification." [11] By early May it began to appear that the weak and vacillating government of Premier Chang Myung would be forced to concede to demands for increased contacts with North Korea.

The Chōsōren propaganda drive was especially successful in its appeal to the youthful followers of Mindan, who, like their counterparts in South Korea, were caught on the lure baited with unification. As a result, Mindan and Chōsōren students cooperated in planning a mass rally for May 17.[12] It seemed that nothing could stop the northern-inspired campaign sweeping Japan.

The Coup of May 16, 1961, in Seoul

Even as this joint student meeting was being planned in Tokyo, forces were at work in Seoul that were to alter the situation in South Korea. Early on the morning of May 16,

[9] *The People's Korea*, April 4, 1961, p. 1.
[10] *Ibid.*, April 25, 1961, p. 3.
[11] *Ibid.*, p. 2. Premier Chang formed his government on August 23, 1960.
[12] *The People's Korea*, May 16, 1961, p. 3.

elements of the South Korean forces staged a coup and seized control of the civil government. The new military government that resulted was violently anticommunist. All talk of cooperation with the north was banned as treasonable, breaking the ban was punishable by death. Neutralistic thought, such as that of Kim Sam-kyu, was severely condemned.[13] The new military government was directed by General Park Chung-hee, a staunch anticommunist and a proponent of a new Korean nationalism. The weak and vacillating regime of Chang Myung had been replaced with a strongly anticommunist government.

The day after the coup in Seoul, the Chōsōren-sponsored meeting of students was held on schedule in Tokyo. Five hundred students issued a joint resolution advocating the unification of Korea, a north-south students' conference, the exchange of students and ideas between the two governments, and the cooperation of all Korean students in Japan.[14] This meeting marked the real end of Chōsōren's almost successful drive to split the ranks of Mindan and destroy that organization. Although many Mindan supporters disapproved of a military government, they rallied behind the new government when they saw that it was following a positive program of reform for South Korea. The coup in Seoul had infused the pro-south movement in Japan with new vigor. On May 31, Mindan displayed this new vigor by sharply reprimanding a group of Mindan-affiliated students who criticized the military government. Mindan director Kwon Il announced to the Japanese press that the students' outburst ran counter to Mindan's decision to support the new government.[15]

The new military government, despite its many problems

[13] Soo Young Lee, *The Revolution in Korea*, p. 7.
[14] *The People's Korea*, May 23, 1961, p. 3.
[15] *The Japan Times*, May 31, 1961, p. 3.

The Unification Issue

at home, began to take action on behalf of the Korean minority in Japan almost from its first week of operation. The government sent a goodwill mission to Japan led by Ambassador Ch'oe Duk-shin — the first such official mission sent to Japan during the postwar period.[16] The new military government adopted a positive program for the minority in Japan. It was concerned especially with the children of school age growing up in Japan. Before the coup government was two months old, two supervisors and ten teachers were sent to Japan to make a survey of educational conditions and needs, and eighty Korean students in Japan were invited to visit South Korea.[17] The Education Ministry of South Korea then began a program to train Korean teachers in Japan. Korean teachers were invited to visit South Korea at government expense, and to be taken on tours of the country. On August 4 the first group of thirty teachers began to attend a series of lectures, sponsored by the Central Education Research Institute. These lectures were intended to explain the revolutionary government's educational policy and give anticommunist instruction. The educators from Japan were to "absorb the message of Korean history, culture, and patriotism for delivery to youthful Koreans in Japan."[18] The new military government considered this project so important that Prime Minister Song Yo-chan personally greeted the visiting teachers at his official residence.[19]

---

[16] Young-dal Ohm, "Problems and Prospects of Korea-Japan Talks," *Korea Journal*, II (April, 1962), 20.

[17] Republic of Korea, *Revolution's First Two Months' Achievements*, p. 18. In all fairness to the Chang Myung government it should be pointed out that South Korea was showing greater interest in Korean education in Japan just before the coup. Chang's government had sent officials of ministerial level to visit schools in Japan. *The Korean Republic*, April 15, 1961, p. 2.

[18] *The Korean Republic Weekly*, August 8, 1962, p. 8.

[19] *The Korean Republic*, August 8, 1961, p. 1.

Besides indoctrinating the teachers with the nationalistic spirit of the new military regime, the government decided to send 261,000,000 won to aid its educational program in Japan. It also planned to build modern school buildings in some Japanese cities and to provide more educational experts to guide the new program.[20]

During the fall of 1961 the military government strengthened its ties with the pro-South Koreans in Japan. In early September, So Sang-yung, who headed the cultural section of the Foreign Office, departed on a three-week lecture tour of Japan to explain the "true nature" of the revolution.[21]

A group of 64 Korean businessmen living in Japan visited South Korea in December at the invitation of General Park. This group, led by Mindan director Kwon Il, pledged its support of South Korea's economic programs. General Park responded by promising that South Korea would do everything possible to advance the interests of the Koreans in Japan. The general informed the visitors that the new military government had created a special agency to deal with the problems of the overseas Koreans.[22] On December 29, as the visitors were departing, Park asked Korean businessmen in Japan for complete cooperation in the economic programs of the new government.[23]

Within the few months after the coup, Park's government had taken a series of important steps to strengthen the ties between South Korea and the Koreans in Japan. This positive approach heartened the followers of Mindan and gave them the spirit to resist the unification drive that Chōsōren was promoting.

[20] *Ibid.*, August 9, 1961, p. 4.
[21] *Ibid.*, September 3, 1961, p. 1.
[22] *Ibid.*, December 23, 1961, p. 1.
[23] *Ibid.*, December 29, 1961, p. 1.

Intensified Political Agitation

On May 23, at its sixth congress, Chōsōren accused the military government of being a "puppet" of the United States. The congress voiced its determination to intensify the drive for unification of the homeland.[24] Two days later, Han Duk-su, chairman of Chōsōren, led a mass rally in Tokyo to condemn the "military fascist dictatorship in South Korea." Representatives from the Japanese Socialist Party, the Japanese Communist Party, and Nitchō Kyōkai joined chairman Han in denouncing the new South Korean government.[25]

During the remainder of 1961 Chōsōren held many meetings in conjunction with Japanese groups to disrupt the negotiations between Japan and South Korea. This movement reached a climax on December 9 at a nationwide rally in Tokyo's Hibiya Park. More than 2,000 Japanese, representing forty political parties and social groups, took part in the rally and the two-hour demonstration through downtown Tokyo.[26]

In a New Year's message for 1962 the central standing committee of Chōsōren reaffirmed its support of North Korean policy, and announced that it would continue to push for the unification of Korea.[27] In mid-January the organization's program for 1962 was outlined in meetings held in Nagoya. Chōsōren urged its members to work hard to rally all Koreans in Japan around the banner of the People's Republic. The program advocated strengthening the educational system, especially in the area of teaching socialist patriotism. To achieve these goals, the Koreans in Japan

[24] *The People's Korea*, May 30, 1961, p. 3.
[25] *Ibid.*
[26] *Ibid.*, December 20, 1961, p. 3.
[27] *Ibid.*, January 1, 1962, p. 1.

must break up diplomatic negotiations between South Korea and Japan.[28]

One of Chōsōren's primary concerns was the development of national education for Korean youths in Japan. The number of Chōsōren-supported schools had risen by 1961 to 320, according to Chōsōren, with an enrollment of about 40,000 students, not counting the 10,000 who had been repatriated to North Korea. Despite the drop in enrollment, Chōsōren estimated that the number of students would again reach 50,000 by April, 1962. The People's Republic, on March 15, sent its tenth grant for educational purposes in the amount of 558,470,000 yen, making a total of 2,101,880,000 yen for educational aid.[29]

The repatriation of Koreans, which had started in December, 1959, was used to good advantage by Chōsōren in its propaganda campaign. The organization claimed that although the vast majority of the Koreans had come originally from South Korea, they now preferred the northern half of the peninsula.[30] The Chōsōren press published letters from the repatriates describing North Korea as a wonderful country full of opportunities. The steady exodus of Koreans continued until it had reached nearly 75,000 by December, 1961. At first, two ships, each carrying 1,500 repatriates were needed to make the short run twice a month. Gradually, however, the number wishing to return deceased, and one ship was dropped from the run. Finally, the North Korean government was forced to propose that the remaining ship make only one trip each month. When the eighty-fifth group of repatriates left Niigata on December 15, only 124 were aboard.[31] The eighty-seventh group,

[28] *Ibid.*, February 21, 1962, p. 3.
[29] *Ibid.*, March 28, 1962, p. 1.
[30] *Ibid.*, January 1, 1962, p. 5.
[31] *The Korean Republic*, December 27, 1961, p. 4.

which sailed in February, 1962, contained only 75 repatriates.[32] Left behind in Japan were approximately 550,000 Koreans who had chosen to remain.

During 1962 and early 1963 both North and South Korea continued to compete for the allegiance of the Korean minority in Japan. Chōsōren extolled Kim Il-sung as the protector of the Koreans in Japan. Because of his concern, Koreans in Japan could live happier lives in Japan and could "act with pride" no matter where they were.[33] In his New Year's message for 1963 Kim Il-sung congratulated Chōsōren on its "brilliant victories" and encouraged it to carry on the struggle for the unification of Korea and the defense of the "national rights" of the Koreans in Japan.[34] The Chōsōren chairman, Han Duk-su, replied to Kim Il-sung by announcing, on March 25, 1963, "Our principal stand on public activities is to base ourselves firmly on the peace-loving foreign policy of North Korea and carry it through."[35]

South Korea responded to the announced plans of the northern regime and Chōsōren by increasing its activities in connection with the minority. General Park called upon the Koreans in Japan to support the revolutionary government in its efforts to rebuild Korea.[36]

In August, 1963, two Japanese delegations, one a Socialist Party group led by Yamamoto Kōichi and the other representing Nitchō Kyōkai, were in Pyongyang to celebrate the fifteenth anniversary of the founding of the People's Republic. Yamamoto told the audience, according to Radio Pyongyang, that "U. S. troops must be expelled from Japan

[32] *Ibid.*, February 14, 1962, p. 4.
[33] *The People's Korea*, April 15, 1962, p. 10.
[34] *Ibid.*, January 9, 1963, p. 1.
[35] *Ibid.*, April 3, 1963, p. 1.
[36] *The Korean Republic Weekly*, August 15, 1962, p. 3.

and the Japan-South Korean normalization talks must be 'frustrated.'" He assailed the policies of the United States in eastern Asia, especially the "plot for the formation of the Northeast Asia military alliance." [37]

Yamamoto's attack on the United States and the Liberal Democratic government in Japan was but a continuation of the Japanese left-wing support for Chōsōren and North Korea. Left-wing political factions in Japan had consistently used the problems of the Koreans in Japan to embarrass the Japanese government. On the other hand, Chōsōren and North Korea had also used the left-wing Japanese organizations.

Toward the end of 1963 the political agitation among the Koreans in Japan increased. The autumn elections for a new president in South Korea, together with the prospect that 1964 would witness a successful completion of the lengthy diplomatic negotiations between Japan and South Korea, encouraged both Chōsōren and Mindan to redouble their efforts to gain the allegiance of the Korean minority in Japan.

[37] *The Asahi Evening News*, September 1, 1963, p. 1. Hatanaka Masaharu led the first Japanese mission to North Korea in May, 1955. Other Japanese groups soon followed his example, and more than a dozen joint agreements were signed between the North Koreans and the Japanese. The flow of Japanese to North Korea so increased that by the spring of 1964 more than a thousand had taken the trip. Kiwon Chung, "Japanese-North Korean Relations Today," pp. 792–793.

XI
THE FUTURE OF THE MINORITY

More than two decades have passed since the end of the Second World War, but the future of the Korean minority in Japan is still uncertain.[1] The troubled relations between them are further complicated by the refusal of North Korea to recognize any agreement to which it is not a party. Repatriation to North Korea, although a diplomatic triumph for the northern regime, has failed to solve the basic problems of the minority or to reduce their numbers substantially. Their economic position has continued

---

[1] Justice Minister Kaya Okinori, speaking on the floor of the Diet on March 30, 1964, commented on the legal status of Korean residents in Japan, "The negotiations on permanent resident status of Koreans have been nearly completed." Kaya continued, "For those South Koreans who came to Japan before the end of the war and lived here until the ratification of the . . . Peace Treaty, permanent residence status will be granted. Their children will be given the same treatment until they reach maturity." In regard to the North Koreans in Japan, he said, "They have at present a de facto permanent residence status. We intend to continue the same treatment for the time being." *The Japan Times*, March 31, 1964, p. 1.

to deteriorate during the past several years, with more unemployment today than in 1952. The number receiving financial aid from the Japanese government has been drastically reduced.[2]

The traditional Japanese dislike for Koreans remains strong, and may even have increased. Bitter and frustrated because of their inferior social position, the Koreans have reciprocated by stressing their nationality. As a result, the politically minded elements among the minority "have a strong feeling of joint solidarity."[3] The Koreans still have no "voice" in the government, and their only means of protest is to be repatriated or to demonstrate in the streets. One spokesman for the minority feels that the Japanese are "gradually driving them into a corner."[4]

Both assimilation and repatriation have failed to solve the minority problem. During the occupation, when the United States military government aided the Japanese in enforcing assimilation, the Koreans reacted by rebelling more violently than they had before the war. The Korean War further inflamed the minority and encouraged the growth of nationalistic political organizations. As a result, the hostility between the two peoples increased. The cause of the problem was not eliminated by removing some of the Koreans from Japan. The effort to repatriate them to North Korea was at best a partial solution.[5]

[2] In 1963 the number of Koreans receiving aid from the government was 59,000. Jun Den, "The 600,000 Orphans," p. 142. The number of Koreans now receiving government aid is very small compared with the total number of people receiving charity payments from the Japanese government. In July, 1963, 660,000 families (1,750,000 people) were receiving livelihood support payments. *Asahi Evening News*, November 5, 1963, p. 3.
[3] Jun Den, "The 600,000 Orphans," p. 140.
[4] *Ibid.*, p. 143.
[5] On December 15, 1963, a group of 114 Koreans, the one hundred and thirteenth group to be repatriated, sailed for Ch'ŏngjin, North

The 1960's: The Nisei Jidai

Even though the problem is yet unsolved, a slightly more hopeful picture is emerging. A subtle but significant change has been taking place in the composition of the Korean minority. The percentage of nisei (second-generation Koreans, born in Japan) is now greater than the percentage of issei (first generation, born in Korea). The nisei majority has, in fact, lost contact with its motherland and is Japanese in speech, customs, and attitudes. Currently 152,600 young Koreans are enrolled from grade school to graduate school, most of them in Japanese schools; only 25,800 are receiving a racial education in the schools of Mindan and Chōsōren. The situation is entirely different from that of a decade ago.[6]

This change is reflected not only in the proportion of nisei to issei but also in the rapid increase in the number of Koreans married to Japanese. In 1952 there were 21,000 mixed families; in 1963 there were more than 30,000.[7] Rel-

---

Korea. This brought to 80,843 the number repatriated since the first group departed from Niigata on December 14, 1959. *The Japan Times*, December 15, 1963, p. 4.

[6] The tabulation classifies the Koreans by age group. The number of Koreans under twenty totals 390,000. All were born in Japan.

Age	Number
Under 10	140,000
10–19	150,000
20–29	100,000
30–39	82,000
40–49	65,000
50 and over	50,000
Total	587,000

See Jun Den, "The 600,000 Orphans," p. 141. The percentage of nisei among the Koreans increased rapidly: in 1930, 8.2 per cent were nisei; in 1950, 49.9 per cent; in 1959, 64.2 per cent. See Hōmushō nyūkoku kanrikyoku hen, *Shutsunyūkoku kanri to sono jittai*, p. 90.

[7] There was a total of 120,000 families. Yu-gan Yi, *A Fifty-Year History of the Koreans in Japan*, p. 142. Den also points out that during

atively few Koreans are active in Korean political organizations. The combined active membership of Mindan and Chōsōren has been estimated at only 70,000 though the two groups claim a total membership of 355,000.[8] The second- and third-generation Koreans are gradually being Japanized. The old Japanese policy of assimilation — the policy that only partially succeeded among the first-generation Koreans — is finally affecting the minority. The process of assimilation, however, can never be fully implemented until the Japanese majority fully accepts the Korean minority as members of Japanese society. A public-opinion poll taken in 1963 shows no lessening of Japanese animosity toward the Koreans.[9] The Japanese government and people must act if they wish to solve the minority problem. The conditions for a lasting solution are available if the Japanese will but take the initiative.

Possible Solutions of the Minority Problem

One Korean historian pointed out that between 300,000 and 400,000 of the Koreans in Japan immigrated in the early 1930's and became permanent residents.[10] This group can be expected to remain in Japan, tenaciously clinging to

recent years an average of 6,000 Koreans per year have been naturalized as Japanese. Jun Den, "The 600,000 Orphans," p. 141. Between April 28, 1952, and the end of 1962 a total of 25,723 Koreans became Japanese citizens. *Shutsunyūkoku* . . . , pp. 91–92. It is interesting to note that about 3,000 Japanese wives accompanied their Korean husbands to North Korea. Hatsuyama, "Arekara nao tsuzuku Kita Chōsen kikoku," *Asahigurafu*, No. 2084 (April 17, 1964), 39.
    [8] Jun Den, "The 600,000 Orphans," p. 142.
    [9] Mitsuharu Mazaki, "Nihonjin no miru Kankoku, Kankokujin no miru Nihon . . . , *Asahi Jānaru* (Asahi Journal), V (December, 1963), 23.
    [10] Kwang chul Rim, "Problems of the Koreans in Japan," *Contemporary Japan*, XXII (1953), 328.

The Future of the Minority

their homes and means of livelihood. Japan's imperial policy during the first half of the twentieth century, made it possible for these Koreans to come to Japan. Now the nation is faced with a minority problem during the second half of the century.

UNESCO, in cooperation with its Japanese branch, conducted an educational experiment designed to lessen prejudice and promote understanding between Japanese and Koreans in Japan. The industrial city of Kawasaki, near Tokyo, which is heavily populated with Koreans, was chosen as the site for the experiment. Sixty Japanese middle-school students, aged thirteen to fourteen, attended special classes for several weeks on the subject of Japanese and Koreans. The Japanese students studied Korean history, geography, culture, and postwar problems. They visited Korean schools and exchanged letters with Korean students. They discussed the basis for prejudice both among themselves and with Korean students. At the end of the program each Japanese student wrote a composition on what he had learned about Korea and the Koreans. The decrease of prejudice among the Japanese students was truly remarkable. The percentage of those who said that they could be friends with Koreans rose from 20 to 70 after the program; those who said that Koreans were "dirty" and could not be accepted as friends dropped from 60 to 10; 20 per cent held a middle view before and after the program.[11]

These results suggest that one way to lessen the animosity between the two peoples is to instruct the young Japanese and Koreans in tolerance. This idea, however good in theory, will be difficult to put into practice. It is doubtful that the Japanese government will encourage many such pro-

[11] Rōdōsha ruporutāju shūdan, *Nihonjin no mita zainichi Chōsenjin*, pp. 43–45. UNESCO, *Education for International Understanding*, pp. 44–46.

grams in Japanese schools. The Korean reaction also must be considered. One Korean teacher, in a Chōsōren-supported school, complained that the Japanese students taking part in the experiment were being taught that Kankoku (the Republic of Korea) was the legal government of the entire peninsula. The teacher reasoned that the program itself was prejudiced and therefore could not possibly destroy prejudice. The Korean educational program is now in an extremely nationalistic phase, perhaps as a reaction to Japan's long-continued suppression of Korean schools. It is unlikely that the Koreans, especially those connected with Chōsōren, will modify their educational program and begin to teach tolerance toward the Japanese.

The UNESCO-sponsored program to teach mutual tolerance in the school system demonstrated that such a plan was feasible. It is up to the Japanese government and the leadership within the minority to promote similar experiments on a larger scale. The Japanese government must, of course, take the first step by establishing special classes in the national school system. It will then be up to the Koreans to complement the government program by introducing a similar one in their private schools. Opposition should gradually decrease as second- and third-generation Koreans gain control of the minority organizations.

Such educational programs may have great value in eliminating prejudice between Koreans and Japanese, but there has also been progress on the diplomatic level. The Japan-South Korea Treaty was signed on June 22, 1965. Its purpose was to establish diplomatic relations between the two countries, and that was done on December 18, 1965. When the treaty was first signed, it triggered political explosions on both sides of the Sea of Japan. Anti-government forces in both countries attempted to use the treaty issue to unseat their opponents. In Japan the treaty drove the socialists and

The Future of the Minority 163

communists into an alliance in both the streets and the Diet, but the leftist-led street demonstrations failed to reach the intensity of those staged five years earlier against the United States-Japan Security Treaty. In the Diet, the greatly outnumbered left-wing coalition could obstruct but not defeat the formal ratification of the new treaty, which was passed by the House of Representatives on November 12, 1965.

One of the agreements attached to the treaty deals directly with the Korean minority living in Japan. The purpose of the agreement is "to provide Korean residents with the means to enjoy a stable life under the Japanese social order." Permanent residence is to be granted to nationals of the Republic of Korea who have continuously lived in Japan since August 15, 1945, and to their descendants who are born by 1970, if applications are made in their name within sixty days after their birth. The Japanese retain the right to deport Koreans who are convicted of serious crimes. The Japanese government is to give "appropriate consideration" to the education, livelihood protection, and national health insurance coverage of the Koreans who qualify under the clauses of the treaty.[12]

The North Korean government and its satellites in Japan responded to the treaty in a predictable manner; they roundly denounced the treaty and refused to accept its provisions. The Foreign Ministry of the Democratic People's Republic of Korea on November 5 charged that the Japanese government was attempting to force all Koreans in Japan to declare themselves South Korean nationals.[13]

Education of Koreans in Japan remains a problem between the government and Chōsōren. During the Upper House debate over the treaty one committee member raised

[12] "Signing of ROK-Japan Treaty and Final Showdown," *One Korea*, No. 46 (July, 1965), 15.
[13] *The People's Korea*, November 10, 1965, p. 1.

the issue of " 'anti-Japanese education being given in some pro-Pyongyang Korean schools.' " The Education Minister replied by saying he was aware of the situation and that the "government will find it inevitable to take action against such schools if it has been proved that they are engaged in anti-Japanese education." [14]

The education and legal or diplomatic levels of change will not affect conditions by themselves. Problems of the Korean minority in Japan are complicated by events outside of that country, for the minority has become deeply involved in the battle between the communist and non-communist world. Any settlement of the status of the minority is therefore closely connected with the settlement of the triangular diplomatic dispute between Japan and the two Koreas. Indeed, a complete solution may not be possible until the entire Korean peninsula has been reunified under one government.

[14] *The Japan Times,* December 5, 1965, p. 2.

BIBLIOGRAPHY

This selective bibliography contains only material cited in the text. In regard to the Japanese language items, especially microfilm and articles in journals, the original English translation has been retained in cases where one was provided.

Documents and Official Publications

Cho, Chung W. *Speeches and Statements by Foreign Minister Chung W. Cho.* Seoul: Ministry of Foreign Affairs, 1959(?).

Chosen. Government-General. *Annual Report on Administration of Chosen. 1918–1921.* Keijo: 1921.

———. *Annual Report on Administration of Chosen. 1922–1923.* Keijo: 1924.

———. *Annual Report on Administration of Chosen. 1926–1927.* Keijo: 1928.

———. *Annual Report on Administration of Tyosen. 1937–1938.* Keijo: 1939.

Chung, Henry (ed.). *Treaties and Conventions between Corea and Other Powers.* New York: H. S. Nichols, Inc., 1919.

Cynn, Hugh. "A Korean View of Pacific Relations," Institute of Pacific Relations, Honolulu Session, June 30–July 14, 1925. Honolulu: 1925.

General Association of Korean Residents in Japan. *For Further Promoting Peaceful Unification of Korea: Material on the Korean Question.* Tokyo: Chosun Shinbo-sa, 1962.

Japan. Consulate General of Japan. Information Office. "Korean Repatriation Agreement Signed," *Japan Report*, V (September, 1959).

———. Gaimushō (Ministry of foreign affairs). Taishō jūyonen chūni okeru zairyū Chōsenjin no jōkyō (The condition of resident Koreans during 1925). Tokyo: 1926. Library of Congress, Reel SP47. Special Studies 155.

———. Hōmushō nyūkoku kanrikyoku hen (Ministry of justice, immigration control bureau). *Shutsunyūkoku kanri to sono jittai* (Immigration control and facts). Tokyo: 1964.

———. Naimushō keihokyoku hoanka (Home ministry, police bureau, security section). *Chōsenjin kankei shorui* (Security matters concerning Koreans). Tokyo: 1941–1942. Library of Congress, Reel 215.

———. ———. *Hokushi jihen ni kansuru jōhō* (Information in connection with the North China incident). Tokyo: 1937. Library of Congress, Reel WT57.

———. ———. *Kyōwa jigyō kankei* (Activities of the Korean-Japanese harmony society). Tokyo: 1944. Library of Congress, Reel 219.

———. ———. *Kyōwakai kankei kaigi shorui shōgakukai kankei o fukumu* (Conferences relating to the Korean-Japanese harmony society). Tokyo: January, 1943. Library of Congress, Reel 217.

———. ———. *Nendobetsu Chōsenjin chiihō ihan kenkyo shirabe sono ta* (Yearly statistics on violations of the peace preservation law by Koreans). Tokyo: 1944–1945. Library of Congress, Reel 222.

———. ———. *Shōwa . . . nenchū ni okeru shakai undō no jōkyō* (The present state of the social movement, 1931–1942). Published annually, 1929–1942.

———. Public Security Investigation Agency. *Current Phases of the Activities of Korean Residents in Japan.* Tokyo: 1957. (In English.)

———. Shihōshō keijikyoku (Ministry of justice, criminal affairs bureau). *Chōsenjin no kyōsanshugi undō* (The Korean Communist movement). Tokyo: 1939.

Kim, Il-sung. "Report at the Celebration Meeting of the Tenth Anniversary of the Founding of the Democratic People's Republic of Korea," *New Korea* (Pyongyang), No. 29 (October, 1958), 20.

Korea [Democratic People's Republic]. *On the Question of the 600,000 Koreans in Japan.* Pyongyang: Foreign Languages Publishing House, 1959.

———. Workers' Party of Korea. *Third Congress of the Workers' Party of Korea: Documents and Materials: April 23–29, 1956.* Pyongyang: Foreign Languages Publishing House, 1956.

Korea [Republic of Korea]. *The Korean Information Bulletin.* Washington: November–December, 1957. Distributed by the Korean embassy.

———. Office of Public Information. Supreme Council for National Reconstruction. *Revolution's First Two Months' Achievements.* Seoul: 1961.

Lee, Soo Young. *The Revolution in Korea: A Report to Our Friends Around the World.* Seoul: Ministry of Public Information, 1962.

United Nations Educational, Scientific, and Cultural Organization. *Education for International Understanding.* Paris: 1959.

United States Strategic Bombing Survey. *The Effects of Strategic Bombing on Japanese Morale.* Washington: 1947.

———. *The Effects of Strategic Bombing on Japan's War Economy.* Washington: 1946.

Books

Allen, Richard C. *Korea's Syngman Rhee: An Unauthorized Portrait.* Tokyo: Charles E. Tuttle Co., 1960.

Asakawa, Kanichi. *The Early Institutional Life of Japan: A Study in the Reform of 645 A. D.* Tokyo: 1903.

Bellah, Robert N. *Tokugawa Religion: The Values of Pre-Industrial Japan.* Glencoe: The Free Press, 1957.

Borton, Hugh. *Japan's Modern Century.* New York: The Ronald Press Co., 1955.

———. *Japan since 1931: Its Political and Social Development.* New York: Institute of Pacific Relations, 1940.

Brown, Delmer M. *Money Economy in Medieval Japan: A Study in the Use of Coins.* Far Eastern Association Monograph No. 1, Institute of Far Eastern Languages. New Haven: Yale University, 1951.

Claude, Inis L., Jr. *National Minorities: An International Problem.* Cambridge: Harvard University Press, 1955.

Cohen, Jerome B. *Japan's Economy in War and Reconstruction.* Minneapolis: University of Minnesota Press, 1949.

Conroy, Hilary. *The Japanese Seizure of Korea: 1868–1910. A Study of Realism and Idealism in International Relations.* Philadelphia: University of Pennsylvania Press, 1960.

Fairbank, John K., Reischauer, Edwin O., and Craig, Albert M. *East Asia the Modern Transformation.* Boston: Houghton Mifflin Co., 1965.

Grajdanzev, Andrew J. *Modern Korea.* New York: International Secretariat, Institute of Pacific Relations. Distributed by the John Day Co., 1944.

Harada, Shuichi. *Labor Conditions in Japan.* New York: Columbia University Press, 1928.

Inui, Kiyo S. *The Unsolved Problem of the Pacific: A Survey of International Contacts, Especially in the Frontier Communities, with Special Emphasis upon California and an Analytic Study of the Johnson Report to the House of Representatives.* Tokyo: The Japan Times, 1925.

Ishii, Ryoichi. *Population Pressure and Economic Life in Japan.* London: P. S. King and Son, Ltd., 1937.

Jorden, William J. "Japan's Diplomacy between East and West," Council on Foreign Relations. *Japan between East and West.* New York: Harper and Brothers, 1957.

Bibliography

Kaigai Jijō Chōsa Hen (Center for the Investigation of Overseas Conditions). *Chōsen yōran* (A survey of Korea). Tokyo: Musashi Shobō, 1960.
Kang, Younghill. *The Grass Roof.* New York: C. Scribner's Sons, 1947.
Kendall, Carlton W. *The Truth about Korea.* San Francisco: The Korean National Association, 1919.
Kim, Sam-kyu. *Chōsen no shinjitsu* (The truth about Korea). Tokyo: Shiseido, 1960.
Kim, San, and Nym Wales. *Song of Ariran.* New York: John Day Co., 1941.
Kim, Suk Hyung, et. al. *On the Grave Errors in the Description on Korea of the "World History" Edited by the U.S.S.R. Academy of Sciences.* Pyongyang: Foreign Languages Publishing House, 1963.
Kuno, Yoshi S. *Japanese Expansion on the Asiatic Continent: A Study in the History of Japan with Special Reference to Her International Relations with China, Korea, and Russia.* Berkeley and Los Angeles: University of California Press, 1940. Vol. II.
Kurzman, Dan. *Kishi and Japan: The Search for the Sun.* New York: Ivan Obolensky, Inc., 1960.
Kyōwakai, Reel 219. See Documents, under Japan, *Kyōwa jigyō kankei.*
Langer, Paul F., and A. Rodger Swearingen. *Japanese Communism: An Annotated Bibliography of Works in the Japanese Language with a Chronology, 1921–1952.* New York: International Secretariat, Institute of Pacific Relations, 1953.
Lee, Chong-sik. *The Politics of Korean Nationalism.* Berkeley and Los Angeles: University of California Press, 1963.
Liem, Channing. *America's Finest Gift to Korea: The Life of Philip Jaisohn.* New York: William-Frederick Press, 1952.
McCune, Evelyn. *The Arts of Korea: An Illustrated History.* Tokyo: Charles E. Tutle Co., 1962.
Mendel, Douglas. *The Japanese People and Foreign Policy: A Study of Public Opinion in Post-Treaty Japan.* Berkeley and Los Angeles: University of California Press, 1961.

Morris, Ivan I. *Nationalism and the Right Wing in Japan: A Study of Postwar Trends.* New York: Oxford University Press, 1960.
Munsterberg, Hugo. *The Arts of Japan: An Illustrated History.* Tokyo: Charles E. Tuttle Co., 1957.
Okochi, Kazuo. *Labor in Modern Japan.* Tokyo: The Science Council of Japan, 1958.
Oliver, Robert T. *Verdict in Korea.* State College, Pennsylvania: Bald Eagle Press, 1952.
Quigley, Harold S. *Japanese Government and Politics: An Introductory Study.* New York: The Century Co., 1932.
Reeve, W. D. *The Republic of Korea: A Political and Economic Study.* London: Oxford University Press, 1963.
Reischauer, Edwin O., and John K. Fairbank. *East Asia the Great Tradition.* Boston: Houghton Mifflin Co., 1958.
Rōdōsha ruporutāju shūdan (Laborers' reporting group). *Nihonjin no mita zainichi Chōsenjin* (Japanese view of the Koreans in Japan). Tokyo: Nihon Kikanshi Tsushinsha, 1959.
Sansom, George. *Japan: A Short Cultural History.* New York: The Century Co., 1931.
―――. *A History of Japan to 1334.* Stanford: Stanford University Press, 1958.
―――. *A History of Japan, 1334–1615.* Stanford: Stanford University Press, 1961.
Scalapino, Robert A. *Democracy and the Party Movement in Prewar Japan.* Berkeley and Los Angeles: University of California Press, 1953.
Shinozaki, Heiji. *Zainichi Chōsenjin undō* (The Korean movement in Japan). Tokyo: Reibunsha, 1953.
Silberman, Bernard S. (ed.). *Japanese Character and Culture: A Book of Selected Readings.* Tucson: The University of Arizona Press, 1962.
Soyeshima, Michimasa. *Oriental Interpretations of the Far Eastern Problem.* Chicago: University of Chicago Press, 1925.
Stoetzel, Jean. *Without the Chrysanthemum and the Sword: A Study of the Attitudes of Youth in Post-War Japan.* New York: Columbia University Press, 1955.
Swearingen, Rodger, and Paul Langer. *Red Flag in Japan: In-*

ternational Communism in Action, 1919–1951. Cambridge: Harvard University Press, 1952.

Taeuber, Irene B. *The Population of Japan*. Princeton: Princeton University Press, 1958.

———. "Population and Labor Force in the Industrialization of Japan, 1850–1950" in Simon S. Kuznets (ed.), *Economic Growth: Brazil, India, Japan*. Durham: Duke University Press, 1955.

Takahashi, Kamekichi. *Nihon sangyō rōdō ron* (A study of Japan's industrial labor). Tokyo: 1937.

Tsunoda, Ryusaku, William Theodore de Bary, and Donald Keene. *Sources of the Japanese Tradition*. New York: Columbia University Press, 1958.

Wagner, Edward W. *The Korean Minority in Japan, 1904–1950*. New York: International Secretariat, Institute of Pacific Relations, 1951.

Weems, Clarence N., Jr. (ed.). *Hulbert's History of Korea*. New York: Hillary House Publishers, 1962.

Wildes, Harry Emerson. *Social Currents in Japan, with Special Reference to the Press*. Chicago: University of Chicago Press, 1927.

Yi, Yu-gan. *A Fifty-Year History of the Koreans in Japan*. See next entry.

———. *Zainichi. Kankokujin no gojūnenshi: hassei ni okeru rekishiteki haikei to kaihogo ni okeru dōkō* (A fifty-year history of the Koreans in Japan: historical background and trends since liberation). Tokyo: Shinkibussan Kabushikigaisha Shuppanbu, 1960.

Yoshino, Sakuzō. "Liberalism in Japan" in K. K. Kawakami (ed.), *What Japan Thinks*. New York: The Macmillan Co., 1921.

Articles

Asakawa, Kanichi. "Japan and Korea," *The Dartmouth Bi-Monthly*, I (1906), 33.

"Assassination of Hara," *Korea Review*, III (November, 1921), 16.

"Assimilation," *Korea Review*, II (August, 1920), 8–9.
Bellah, Robert N. "Japan's Cultural Identity: Some Reflections on the Work of Watsuji Tetsuro," *The Journal of Asian Studies*, XXIV (August, 1965), 573–594.
Chung, Kiwon. "Japanese-North Korean Relations Today," *Asian Survey*, IV (April, 1964), 788–803.
Clark, C. A. "The Korean Church in Japan," *The Japan Christian Quarterly*, VII (July, 1932), 264.
Colegrove, Kenneth. "Labor Parties in Japan," *The American Political Science Review*, XXIII (May, 1929), 359.
Conde, David. "The Korean Minority in Japan," *Far Eastern Survey*, XVI (February, 1947), 41.
Conroy, Hilary. "Chōsen Mondai: The Korean Problem in Meiji Japan," *Proceedings of the American Philosophical Society*, C (1956), 445.
Den, Jun. "Rokujūmannin no minashigo, Amerika ni okeru kokujin no sonzai ni mo hisubeki rokujūman no zainichi Chōsenjin mondai ni me o tojite wa naranu" (The 600,000 orphans: we must not close our eyes to the problem of the 600,000 Koreans living in Japan which is similar to that of the Negroes in America), *Bungei Shunju*, XLI (October, 1963), 140–148.
Dionisopoulos, R. Allan. "Japanese-Korean Relations: A Dilemma in the Anti-Communist World," *Midwest Journal of Political Science*, I (May, 1957), 61.
"Employment Continues Upward," *The Oriental Economist*, III (May, 1936), 294.
Fujishima, Unai, Kunio Maruyama, and Hyōe Murakami. "Zainichi Chōsenjin rokujūmannin no genjitsu" (The actuality of the 600,000 Koreans in Japan), *Chūō Kōron* (Central Review), LXXIII (December, 1958), 191.
Haratani, Tatsuo. "Minzokuteki sutereotaipu to kōaku kanjō ni tsuite no kōsatsu" (Study on stereotypes and preferences among Japanese students toward themselves and other national and ethnic groups), *Kyōiku Shinrigaku Kenkyū* (Japanese Journal of Educational Psychology), VIII (June, 1960), 1–7.

Bibliography

Hardie, R. A. "Koreans in Japan," *The Korean Mission Field*, XXI (June, 1925), 121.
Hatsuyama, [?]. "Arekara nao tsuzuku Kita Chōsen kikoku" (The repatriation to North Korea still continues), *Asahigurafu* (Asahi Picture News), No. 2084 (April 17, 1964), 39.
Idei, Seishi, "The Unemployment Problem in Japan," *International Labour Review*, XXII (October, 1930), 510.
"Independence Movement in Japan," *Korea Review*, I (May, 1919), 84–85.
International Committee of the Red Cross. "The International Committee and the Repatriation of Koreans Resident in Japan," *Revue Internationale de la Croix-Rouge*, Supplement, XIII (April, 1960), 63–68.
"Japanese Imperialism and Aggression: Reconsiderations. I.," *The Journal of Asian Studies*, XXII (August, 1963), 469–472.
Kawakami, K. K. "Japan's Policy toward Alien Immigration," *Current History*, XX (June, 1924), 473.
Kim, Tu-yang. "Chōsenjin undō wa tenkan shitsutsu aru" (The Korean movement is changing), *Zen-ei* (Vanguard), I (May 1, 1947), 38.
"The Korean Nationalist Movement," *Korea Review*, I (August, 1919), 15.
"Koreans in Japan (1)," *Korea Journal* (Seoul), II (April, 1962).
"Koreans in Japan (2)," *Korea Journal*, II (May, 1962), 50.
Kuzutani, Takamasa. "Minzokuteki Kōaku to sono jinkakuteki akuin" (Interracial preferences and their personality determinants), *Kyōiku Shinrigaku Kenkyū* (Japanese Journal of Educational Psychology), VIII (June, 1960), 8–17.
―――. "Shominzoku ni taisuru kōaku taido no kenkyū" (A study of the Japanese attitudes of likes and dislikes toward various nationalities), *Kyōiku Shinrigaku Kenkyū* (Japanese Journal of Educational Psychology), III (July, 1955), 39–57.
"Labor in Time of War," *The Oriental Economist*, VIII (August, 1941), 405.
"Labor Shortage and Walkouts," *The Oriental Economist*, IV (May, 1937), 263.
"Labor Supply Shortage," *The Oriental Economist*, Supplement, August, 1938, pp. 18–19.

Ladd, George Trumbull. "The Annexation of Korea: An Essay in 'Benevolent Assimilation,' " *The Yale Review*, New Series, I (1911–1912), 655.
Lee, In Ha, and Jean E. Sonnenfeld. "Koreans in Japan: Conflict or Reconciliation?" *The Japan Christian Quarterly*, XXV (October, 1959), 301.
Lee, Jin Won. "Brief Survey of Korean-Japanese Relations (Post-War Period)," *Koreana Quarterly* (Seoul), I (Autumn, 1959), 65.
Matsuo, Takayoshi. "Kantō daishinsai moto no Chōsenjin gyakusatsu jiken" (The slaughter of the Koreans during the Great Kantō Earthquake), *Shisō* (Thought), Part I, No. 471 (September, 1963), 44–61.
Mazaki, Mitsuharu. "Nihonjin no miru Kankoku, Kankokujin no miru Nihon. . . . ryōkoku de okonawareta chōsa o tegakari ni . . ." (Japanese view of Korea, Korean view of Japan. . . . A clue from investigations in both countries . . .), *Asahi Jānaru* (Asahi Journal), V (December, 1963), 20–25.
Minami, Jiro. "Japanese-Korean 'Fusion' Said Vital to Creation of New Order in East Asia," *The China Weekly Review*, August 19, 1939, p. 379.
Mitarai, Tatsuo. "Korean-Japan Diplomacy," *The Oriental Economist*, XXVI (April, 1958), 190.
Nihon kindaishi jiten. See Yearbooks and Dictionaries.
Ninomiya, Shigeaki. "An Inquiry Concerning the Origin, Development, and Present Situation of the *Eta* in Relation to the History of Social Classes in Japan," *Transactions of the Asiatic Society of Japan*, X, Second Series (December, 1933), 69–70.
Ohm, Young-dal. "Problems and Prospects of Korea-Japan Talks," *Korea Journal*, II (April, 1962), 20.
Ono, Kazuichiro. "The Problem of Japanese Emigration," *Kyoto University Economic Review*, XXVIII (April, 1958), 47.
"Overpopulation and Immigration in Japan," *The Living Age*, CCCXVI (February 10, 1923), 315.

Bibliography

Red Cross. See International Committee of the Red Cross.
Rim, Kwang chul. "Problems of the Koreans in Japan," *Contemporary Japan*, XXII (1953), 328.
Scalapino, Robert A. and Chong-sik Lee. "The Origins of the Korean Communist Movement (II)," *The Journal of Asian Studies*, XX (February, 1961), 164.
"Signing of ROK-Japan Treaty and Final Showdown," *One Korea*, No. 46 (July, 1965), 15.
Taeuber, Irene B. "The Population Potential of Postwar Korea," *The Far Eastern Quarterly*, V (May, 1946), 298–299.
Tamaki, Motoi. "Nihon Kyōsantō no zainichi Chōsenjin shidō" (The Japan Communist party and the Korean residents in Japan — how the former led the latter), *Koria Hyōron* (Korea Review), No. 38 (April, 1961), 26.
Ubukata, Naokichi. "Nihonjin no Chōsen kan" (The Japanese view of Korea), *Shisō* (Thought), No. 448 (October, 1961), 1265.
"A War of Coal," *The Oriental Economist*, XI (April, 1944), 167–168.
Wildes, Harry E. "Japan's Struggle for Democracy," *The World Tomorrow*, VIII (June, 1925), 174–176.
Yi Kwang-su. "What Christianity Has Done for Korea," *Missionary Review of the World* (New York), Old Series, XLI (August, 1918), 607.
Yoshio, Eisuke. "Chōsenjin no naichi tokō" (Korean migration to Japan), *Gaikō Jihō* (Diplomatic Review), LIII (March 15, 1930), 175.
Yoshisaka, Shunzo. "Labour Recruiting in Japan and Its Control," *International Labour Review*, XII (July, 1925), 488.
Young, R. L. "Koreans in Japan," *The Korean Mission Field*, XXXII (April, 1936), 69.

Yearbooks and Dictionaries

Green, D. G. (ed.). *The Christian Movement in Japan*. Tokyo: Kyō Bun Kwan, 1907.
Kyoto daigaku bungakubu kokushi kenkyūshitsu hen (National

history research division, department of literature, Kyoto University). *Nihon kindaishi jiten* (A dictionary of modern Japanese history). Tokyo: Tōyō Keizai Shinpōsha, 1958.
Sekai daihyakka jiten. (A large world encyclopedia). Tokyo: Heibonsha, 1957.
Shakai Undō Chōsakai Hen (Committee for the Investigation of the Social Movement). *Sayoku dantai jiten.* (A dictionary of left-wing organizations). Tokyo Musashi Shōbo, 1961.
Takenobu, Y. (ed.). *The Japan Yearbook, 1917.* Tokyo: 1917.
———. *The Japan Yearbook, 1919–20.* Tokyo: 1920.
———. *The Japan Yearbook, 1924–25.* Tokyo: 1925.
———. *The Japan Yearbook, 1928.* Tokyo: 1928.

Newspapers and Journals

The Asahi Evening News, 1963.
The Japan Chronicle, 1938.
The Japan Times, 1961–1965.
Korea Journal (Seoul), 1962.
Korea Review (Philadelphia), 1919–1921.
The Korean Repository (Seoul), 1896.
The Korean Republic (Seoul), 1961–1962.
The Korean Republic Weekly, 1962–1963.
The Korean Review (Seoul), 1905.
The New York Times, 1959–1960.
The People's Korea (Tokyo), 1961–1965.
Trans-Pacific (Tokyo), 1923–1939.

Unpublished Materials

Lee, Chong-sik. "The Korean Nationalist Movement, 1905–1945." Unpublished doctoral dissertation, University of California, Berkeley, 1961.
Weems, Clarence N., Jr. "The Korean Reform and Independence Movement (1881–1898)." Unpublished doctoral dissertation, Columbia University, 1954.

INDEX

Aikoku Seinen Kai (Patriotic Youth Association). *See* Korean Nationalist movement
Ainu, 3
Akahata (Red Flag). *See* Newspapers
Annexation of Korea (August 22, 1910): uprisings, 12; military rule, 12; causing migration of Koreans, 27
Army coup (February 26, 1936). *See* Korean Nationalist movement
Assimilation: of early immigrants by the Japanese, 3; policy after August, 1919, 23–24; official policy, 90–91; election law of 1925, language problem, 96; magnitude of problem, 97; failure, 98; affecting the minority, 160

Berlin Olympic Games (1936). *See* Korean Nationalist movement
Buddhism, 1–3

Chang Myung, 149, 150
China: T'ang in Korea, 2; Japanese embassies to, 4
Cho Chung-whan, 141, 143
Ch'oe Duk-shin, 151

Ch'oe Nam-sŏn, 20
Chōren. *See* Zainichi Chōsenjin Renmei
Chōsen Chūō Geijutsu Dan (Korean Central Art Group), 124
Chōsen Chūritsu Undō Iinkai (Korean Committee for the Neutralization of Korea), 127
Chōsen Daigaku (Korea University). *See* Chōsoren
Chōsen Kenkoku Sokushin Seinen Dōmei (Korean Youth League to Promote the Construction of the State), 106–107
Chosen Kyōsantō Nihon Sōkyoku (Korean Communist party, Japan General Bureau), 56
Chōsen Mondai (Korea problem), 7
Chōsen Mondai Kenkyūjo (Korea Problems Research Center), 124
Chōsen Musansha Shakai Renmei (Korean Proletarian Social League), 36
Chōsen Rōdō Sōdōmei (Korean Federation of Labor), 51, 52
Chōsen Shōgakukai (Korean Study Aid Association), 73
Chōsen Tsūshin (Korean News). *See* Newspapers
Chōsen Tsūshinsha (Korean News Agency), 122
Chōsenjin Mondai Kyōgikai (Korean Problems Conference Association). *See* Korean Nationalist Movement
Chōsōren. *See* Zainichi Chōsenjin Sōrengōkai
Chūō Kyōwakai (Central Concordia Association). *See* Kyōwakai
Confucian system, 4, 7

Dai Nippon Rōdōkumiai Sōdōmei Yūaikai (Grand Japan Federation of Labor Unions Fraternal Association, 35
"Dangerous thought," 57, 59, 70, 73
Democratic Peoples Republic of Korea, 116, 136–140, 147, 154, 156, 163

Education. *See* Chōren, Chōsōren, Mindan, SCAP
Emperor of Japan: attempted assassination, 67; announces Koreans equal to Japanese, 93

Farm tenancy, 27
Fukuzawa Yukichi, 7, 8

Index

Gakushū Shobō, 123
Government-general of Korea. *See* Korean immigrants
Great Earthquake. *See* Kantō Dai Shinsai

Hagu-hoe (Student Fraternal Association), 18, 19
Han Duk-su (leader of Chōsōren), 122, 149, 153, 155
Hara Kei, 24-26
Hatanaka Masaharu, 124, 125, 140, 148
Higashikuni Naruhiko, 111
Hirasawa Keichi, 40
Hokuseikai (North Star Society), 53. *See also* Korean Communist movement

Ichigatsukai (January Society): and Japanese members, 34-35; and the March First ceremony of 1925, 51; and the memorial service for Korean victims of the earthquake, 52; a left-wing group, 54
Ii Yashiro, 148
Ikeda Hayato, 148
Inukai Tsuyoshi, 67
Invasion, 5, 6
Ishibashi Tanzan, 110
Itō Hirobumi (resident-general at Seoul), 10, 11, 12
Iwasa Sakutarō, 34
Izumi Ippan Rōdō Kumiai (Izumi General Labor Association). *See* Korean Nationalist movement
Izumi Seiichi, 133

Japan-South Korea Treaty, 162-163. *See also* Japanese relations with Republic of Korea
Japanese anti-Korean campaign, 109-110
Japanese Communist movement: Red scare, 48; early leftwing thought groups, 53-54; Nihon Kyōsantō, 60; illegal organization of Zenkyō in 1928, 60; cooperation with Korean Communists, 60; first official platform, 60; "nationalities policy" of the central committee, 61; Korean membership in

Zenkyō in 1933, 61; policy toward Korean Communists, 64; Korean members and discrimination, 94; policy toward Korean minority after August, 1945, 115–116; organized Kobe riots, 116; ties with Minsen, 120; connection with Chōsōren, 121; supporting Chōsōren rally, 148–149
Japanese immigration: policy of the government, 41, 44–46, 76; Japanese divided on, 41; laws, 42; attitude of industry and labor, 43; demands for cheap labor, 46; new regulations of 1943, 73; and the war effort, 75; restrictions, 82–83; comprehensive regulations in 1942, 83; illegal, 86
Japanese land survey of 1910–1918, 28
Japanese relations with Republic of Korea, 134–136, 145. See Repatriation
Japanese Society, 6, 90–91
Japanese students, 22
Japanese view of Koreans: 13, 26, 31–34, 38, 40, 67, 80, 88, 92, 101; public-opinion polls 1951–1959, 132–133; public-opinion poll of 1963, 160

Kaneko Ayako, 35
Kanemitsu Hososako, 149
Kantō Dai Shinsai (the Great Kantō Earthquake), 38–41, 52
Katō Kōmei, 44
Kaya Okinori, 157
Kazama Jōkichi, 60
Kenseikai (Constitutional party), 144
Kim Ch'i-jŏng, 61, 64–65
Kim Ch'ŏn-hae (Kin Ten-kai), 55, 106, 117
Kim Il, 143
Kim Il-sung, 120, 128, 138, 140, 155
Kim Ku, 67
Kim Ok-kyun, 7, 8, 10
Kim Sam-kyu, 127, 150
Kishi Nobusuke, 141, 143, 144
Kokudokai (National Society), 36
Kokutokai (Black Wave Association), 34
Konno Yōjirō, 64

Index

Kōrai Kyōsan Seinenkai Nihonbu (Korean Communist Youth Society, Japan Section, 56
Korea problem, 10. *See also* Chōsen Mondai
Korean Communist movement: proto-communist groups, 53–55; connection with Japanese, 54, 60–61; membership, 55–56; illegal part of organization, 56; Zenkyō used to rebuild the party, 61; unified movement, 62; rally of Rōsō, old Rōsō dissolved, 62; growth of Zenkyō, 62–63; first official party in Seoul, 63; rebuilding the party in Korea, 65; failure of prewar movement, 66; postwar cooperation with Japanese, 101, 120–121. *See also* Kim-Ch'i-jŏng
Korean military service, 71, 87
Korean minority: treatment by the Japanese 2–3; size before 1920, 14; migration after 1910, 28; jobs and labor, 29; illiteracy, 30; winter relief projects, 31; disputes over housing, 33; disagreements with Japanese, 34; supported by Japanese labor, 35; peace and friendship associations, 37; results of Great Kantō Earthquake, 41; not the cause of unemployment, 46; gains in the 1920's, 47; and Korean nationalists, 49; permanent nature of, 76–77; change in composition after 1939, 77; need for Korean labor, 77; and Labor Mobilization Law of 1939, 78; and government-general, 79; and laborers, 79–85; attracted to Japan, 86; legal status, 89, 119, 157, 163; disputes with Japanese, 92–93; Emperor announces Koreans equal, 93; in politics, 94–95; as a liberated people, 109; riots, 112; registration in Osaka, 112; May Day riots of 1952, 120; political organizations, 121; clustered settlements, 126; Livelihood Protection Law, 130; registration and politics, 130; political activities, 145; financial aid, 158; percentage of nisei and issei, 159; tabulation by age group, 159; marriages to Japanese, 159; active in political groups, 160; UNESCO experiment, 161; solution for the problem, 161–162
Korean Nationalist movement: 50–51; cooperation with the communists, 66; Manchurian Incident, 66; attempt on life of Emperor, 67; army coup of February 26, 1936 and Berlin Olympic Games, 69; Chōsenjin Mondai Kyōgikai organized in Kyoto, 69; Aikoku Seinen Kai, 69; Izumi Ippan Rōdō

182 *Index*

Kumiai, 69; illegal school in Sakai, 70; the North China Incident, 70; seditious slogans, 71; cooperation with Japanese, 71; patriotism not durable, 74. *See also* Subversive activity
Korean population in Japan, 28, 76–77, 131
Korean Provisional Government, 25, 51, 66, 67
Korean reformers. *See* Kim Ok-kyun, Pak Yŏng-hyo
Korean students, 8, 10, 14–21, 49, 51, 57, 63, 73, 129, 150, 151, 154, 159, 161; in 1925, 30; relations with landlords, 33; organize Hokuseikai, 53; and the military, 71; communist education in Chōren schools, 127; headed unification drive in Seoul, 149. *See also* Kim Ok-kyun, Fukuzawa Yukichi
Koria Hyōron (Korea Review), 127. *See also* Kim Sam-kyu
Kumase, 3
Kwon Il, 150, 152
Kyongsang Province, 9
Kyōwa Jigyō. *See* Kyōwakai, Sōaikai
Kyōwakai (Concordia Association), 71–73, 80, 82, 84, 88, 96
Kyōwa Shinbun. *See* Kyowakai

Labor Mobilization Law. *See* Korean immigrants
Livelihood Protection Law, 130. *See also* Korean minority

Manchurian Incident (1931). *See* Korean Nationalist movement
March First movement (1919), 15, 19, 21–25, 51
Matoda Sakunoshin, 46
May Day: 1924, 36; 1925, 37; 1952, 120
Min, Queen, 10
Minami Jirō, 97
Mindan. *See* Zainichi Daikanminkoku Kyoryūmindan
Minobe Tatsukichi, 17

Nam Il, 137
National General Mobilization Act, 78
New Dehli Conference (1955), 124
Newspapers: *Kokumin* on Korean labor, 43; *JiJi Shinpō* and immigration policy, 43; *Osaka Mainichi* and immigration, 44–45; *JiJi Shinpō*'s defense of immigration, 46; *Akahata*

Index 183

propaganda among Koreans, 61; *Asahi* and Korean labor, 78; *Kyōwa Shinbun*, 82; *Tokyo Mainichi*, 109; *Akahata* ceases publication, 117; *Chōsen Tsūshin* as part of Chōsōren network, 123
Nihon Kyōsantō (Japanese Communist party). *See* Japanese Communist movement
Nihon Rōdō Sōdōmei, 36
Nihon Rōdō Hyōgikai (Japan Labor Union Council), 35
Nippon Rōdō Kumiai Zenkoku Kyōgikai, or Zenkyō (National Conference of Japanese Trade Unions), 60. *See also* Japanese Communist movement
Nitchō Bōeki Kai (Japanese-Korean Trade Society), 124
Nitchō Kyōkai (Japanese-Korean Society), 124, 125, 139, 143
North China Incident (1937). *See* Korean Nationalist movement
Nozaka Sanzō, 149

Obon (Festival of the Dead), 76
Ono Tomemutsu, 110
Osugi Sakae, 40

Paekche, 2
Pak Ch-un-gŭm (Pak Shun-kin), 94
Pak Un-sik, 18
Pak Yŏl (Boku Retsu), 34, 106
Pak Yŏng-hyo, 7
Park Chung-hee, 146, 150, 152, 155
Peace Preservation Law. *See* Subversive activity
Piracy, 5

Repatriation, 101–105, 139, 141–144, 159
Republic of Korea: political and economic conditions, 145; fall of Rhee government, 146; unification drive, 149; coup of May 16, 1961, 149–150; new anticommunist government, 150; help for the minority, 151; educational program, 152; increased activities, 155; presidential elections of 1963, 156;

Japan-South Korean Treaty, 162–163. *See also* Japanese relations with Republic of Korea
Rhee Syngman. *See* Syngman Rhee
Rōdō Kaikyū (Labor Class). *See* Newspapers
Rōdō Kaikyūsha (Labor Class Association), 64–65. *See also* Kim Ch'i-jŏng
Rōdō Nomintō (Labor-Farmer party), 35
Rōsō. *See* Zainichi Chōsen Rōdō Sōdōmei

Saitō Makoto, 23, 24, 42, 43
Sakuradamon Incident (January 8, 1932). *See* Korean Nationalist movement
San Francisco Treaty of Peace, 119, 128
Sanichi Musan Seinenkai (March-First Proletarian Youth Society), 53–55
SCAP, 100–102, 107–117
Schools, 15. *See also* Chōren, Chōsōren, Mindan, SCAP
Sekiya Teizaburō, 72
Shiikuma Saburō, 110
Shin Chōsen Kensetsusha Dōmei (League of Founders of the New Korea), 106
Shinjinkai (New Man's Society), 18
Shinseikai (New Star Society), 35
Sōaikai (Mutual Love Society), 38
So Sang-yung, 152
Song Yo-chan, 151
Special Higher Police (Tokkō Keisatsu). *See* Subversive activity
Subversive activity: 56–59, 64–71, 116, 117, 123; students, 20; and March First movement, 26, 152; and the Great Kantō Earthquake, 38–41; and Japanese government, 48; and police blacklist, 49; and Korean communists, 50; and Peace Preservation Law, 52; during the war, 86–87; and SCAP, 101; Koreans as a security problem, 116; world situation caused tensions, 117; creation of a special investigation bureau, 117; communist education, 123
Supreme Commander for the Allied Powers. *See* SCAP
Syngman Rhee, 25, 125, 135–139, 143, 146

Taehan Hunghak-hoe (Greater Korean Promotion of Education Association), 18
Takatsu Masamichi, 54
Tanaka Giichi, 59
Terauchi Masatake (first governor-general of Korea), 12
Three Kingdoms, 2, 4
Tokkō Keisatsu. See Subversive activity
Tokugawa Ieyasu, 6
Tonghak Rebellion, 9
Toyotomi Hideyoshi, 5, 6, 9
Treaty of Kanghwa (1876), 8, 9
Tsuruhara, 11
Tsushima, 6

Unemployment, 29. See also Korean minority
UNESCO educational experiment, 161. See Korean minority
Unified communist movement, 62
United States-Japan Security Treaty, 163

Wilson, Woodrow, 19, 25

Yamamoto Kōichi, 155–156
Yamato clan, 1–3
Yanagi Sōetsu, 23
Yangban (local gentry), 28
Yi dynasty, 7
Yi Kwang-su, 15, 16, 19, 21, 25
Yi Pong-ch'ang (Asayama Shōichi), 67
Yoshida Shigeru, 117–118
Yoshino Sakuzō, 17, 22–23
Yun Keun, 106

Zainichi Chōsen Tōitsu Minshū Sensen, or Minsen (Korean United Democratic Front in Japan), 118, 120, 121
Zainichi Chōsenjin Kikoku Kyōryoku Kai (Cooperation Society for the Repatriation of Korean Nationals in Japan), 124. See also Repatriation

Zainichi Chōsenjin Renmei, or Chōren (League of Koreans in Japan), 104–106, 114–116. *See also* Repatriation

Zainichi Chōsenjin Shōrengōkai (Association of Korean Businessmen in Japan), 124

Zainichi Chōsenjin Sōrengōkai, or Chōsōren (General Federation of Korean Residents in Japan): 121–123, 126–129; funds from DPRK, 138, 154; unification drive, 145; promoted DPRK's unification plan, 147–148; mass rally of students, 149–150; sixth congress, 153; New Year's message for 1962, 163; number of schools and students, 154; reaction to UNESCO's experiment, 162; anti-Japanese education, 164

Zainichi Daikanminkoku Kyoryūmindan, or Mindan (Community of Korean Residents in Japan): established in 1948, 106–107; school system, 114; volunteers for ROK army, 120; organization and membership, 125–126; schools, 128–129; students hold a rally with Chōsōren, 149–150

Zainihon Chōsen Rōdō Sōdōmei, or Rōsō (Federation of Labor of the Koreans in Japan), 36, 55. *See also* the Korean communist movement

Zainihon Chōsen Seinen Dōmei (Korean Youth League in Japan), 56

Zenkoku Suiheisha (National Leveling League), 36, 48